The Struggle for Literacy

Irving Lee Rother, Ph.D.

DETSELIG
ENTERPRISES LTD

The Struggle for Literacy
© 2008 Irving Lee Rother.

Library and Archives Canada Cataloging in Publication
    Rother, Irving Lee
        The struggle for literacy / Irving Lee Rother.

    Includes bibliographical references.
    ISBN 978-1-55059-351-8

    1. Media literacy. 2. Literacy programs. 3. Students with social
    disabilities--Education (Secondary). 4. Alternative education. 5. Mass
    media in education. 6. Media programs (Education). I. Title.

LC4086.R68 2008   373.133   C2008-905033-9

DETSELIG ENTERPRISES Ltd

210 1220 Kensington Road NW
Calgary, Alberta   T2N 3P5
www.temerondetselig.com
temeron@telusplanet.net
p. 403-283-0900   f. 403-283-6947

We recognize the support of the Government of Canada through the
Book Publishing Industry Development Program (BPIDP) for our
publishing program.

We also acknowledge the support of the Alberta Foundation for the Arts
for our publishing program.

SAN 113-0234
ISBN 978-1-55059-351-8
Printed in Canada

Cover Design by James Dangerous

Dedicated to my sons, David & Jesse, my wife Lucie,
co-teacher Aggie, and to Winston.

I would also like to acknowledge the students of
the Alternative Education Program.

TABLE OF CONTENTS

INTRODUCTION

In his book, *The End of Education*, Neil Postman writes "the purpose of a narrative is to give meaning to the world, not to describe it scientifically" (p. 7). I intend to tell the story of the students and I in the *Alternative Career Education Program* (ACE) over several years, as they participated in a Media Literacy curriculum, which I designed. With this in mind, this book is a narrative, which suggests that much of this book is written in the first person point of view.

Dewey (1929) reminds us that inquiry starts with self doubt and moves toward resolving these doubts; and that reflective thinking liberates us from impetuous and routine activities. Dewey's words hit a chord with me. I realized early in my career that if I were to grow as a teacher, I would need to break away from traditional practices, which frankly bored me as a high school student, and frustrated me as a teacher. In many ways, I hope that my writing this book will confirm not only my own understandings about literacy and Media Literacy, but also about ideas around learning and teaching. I hope to challenge traditional teaching practices and beliefs, while supporting and igniting interest in non traditional approaches, such as Media Education Curriculum and Pedagogy.

Graduates of faculties of education in the province of Quebec in 1977 were fairly optimistic about securing a teaching position; that is, unless you were a Fine Arts major, as I was. After several months and numerous interviews, I realized that the teaching of Art was not a priority in the Quebec curriculum. However, Special Education was in its infancy during the mid to late 1970s, and the demand for trained teachers in that area was growing.

On one hand, I had only a vague notion what Special Education was about. On the other hand, I was determined not to let three years of teacher education fade away. Consequently, I soon found myself enrolled in a Special Education diploma program at Montreal's McGill University. As fate would have it, within a week of registering, I was hired as a Special Education teacher at a local high school.

However, the novelty of teaching soon wore off. By 1979, I was beginning to become disillusioned with traditional teaching. While I still had the desire to teach, I considered the methods, materials and evaluation procedures that I was using in my Special Education English Language Arts classes as little more than the repackaging and reformatting of commercial learning materials which the students had negatively experienced in previous years, and which for the most part confirmed their previous failures in learning the material.

The methods I was using were no different from any other Special Education class I had observed. I stood at the front of the room, barked out questions, wrote on the black board, while the students sat in rows, draped over their desks, as they mechanically copied what I had written. The reading materials I used were what was then described as "high interest, low vocabulary," although they rarely seemed to spark any interest in my students. Frankly, I too was bored by the material. The written material was something I had usually watered down from a teacher's reference book and/or guide, and which I mimeographed. The audio visual resources I used were most often 1960 and 1970 produced educational documentaries, not exactly the most stimulating materials for students already turned off by schooling in general. And the technology I used, if at all, was an overhead projector and 16 mm film projector.

As per standard operating procedures for Special Education class evaluations, I administered a standardized reading test at the beginning, middle and end of the school year. Often, it seemed that there was an incongruity between the intended goals of my remedial English Program, designed to improve basic literacy skills, and the student scores reflected in standardized reading tests. I learned to rationalize my students' very poor results on these standardized reading test. That is, I congratulated myself when a student's score improved, even minimally, and ignored scores when the students did not improve, or worse, seemed to slip backward, which I attributed to the fact that it was the end of the school year, and that they had other things on their minds.

"Worthless Chatter?"

What I could not ignore was the lack of my students' involvement, interest, and motivation. At first, I accepted their apathy as a traditional dislike of schooling, and as a defense mechanism against academic failure. However, the behavior that continually offended me was that they seemed to have lost that natural sense of curiosity and enthusiasm for learning that we expect in youth. They did not feel a part of what was going on in the classroom. They deliberately absented their intelligence, effort, and interest from my classroom. Their bodies were there, but not much else. I recall being annoyed and distracted because they were talking to each other about the latest television soap opera, situation comedy, or fictional program, when they should have been concentrating on the work that I had assigned. Not a day went by that they were not discussing – in detail – the latest episode of not just one, but several television programs.

The more I listened to this "worthless chatter", the more I began to realize that there was something exciting in the way they were talking about the television programs, movies and/or videos that they watched outside of classroom. They knew the characters and plots well. But what was really interesting was the sophistication of their conjectures, plot analyses and predictions, a sophistication that never appeared when they were asked to analyze the short paperback novels that I assigned. Maybe their ability to recall and infer issues related to their television viewing, was not so unique in and of itself, but as a relatively novice teacher, the level of their discussions caught me by surprise.

Defining Moment

In 1986, I was in the final stages of my Master's thesis, *Using Video as a Process Tool with Learning Disabled and Emotionally Disturbed Adolescents* (Rother, 1986). Although I did not realize it then, my Master's thesis was to become a defining moment in my thinking about at-risk students, learning, teaching, literacy, and media.

My Master's thesis presented the format for the design and production of student produced video material as a means of increasing the special education students' understanding of themselves and their interpersonal relationships. It was not intended as a media curriculum. While the results of my master's research were statistically significant, it was the 'unexpected' that I found most exciting.

"I Can't Watch TV Anymore!"

In the last few weeks of collecting my data for my Master's thesis, I began to question the often labeled "low level of literacy" characteristics of my students. My students and I had been using a portable television studio – including two cameras, a switcher, and audio equipment, – to reenact specific incidents in their lives. During one of our taping sessions, Ron, one of the boys in the class, approached me after class, at which time the following conversation, paraphrased below, occurred:

> **Ron:** Since we started taping, I can't watch television anymore! It's not the same.
> **Me:** I don't understand.
> **Ron:** I mean, I was watching a program last night, and it was all wrong!
> **Me:** How?
> **Ron:** OK, they had this girl crying and they used a long shot.
> **Me:** So? What's wrong with that?
> **Ron:** She was crying. It was emotional.
> **Me:** What kind of shot would you have used?
> **Ron:** A close up. Then you could see her face, you know crying.

Keeping in mind that Ron was seventeen years old, and reading around the grade three level; he went on to graphically critique the television program in greater detail, and to describe how he would have shot and edited it. What is even more surprising is that beyond a fundamental understanding of some basic television production vocabulary, I had not taught the students television grammar or production techniques. That is, Ron's rather sophisticated learning came from his own "reading" of a television program. As incredible as it now seems, and as inexcusable as it feels, I am not sure I ever seriously considered what students learned about media outside of my class as having much relevance to what we did in school. If anything, I probably considered such distractions interference to what I was attempting to teach.

It was not just what Ron said, but how he said it that intrigued me. He was excited and eager to show what he understood about camera shots, and how he would have rewritten the presentation of the scene. The conversation with Ron prompted me to ask other students in the class about their understandings of the media texts they watched outside of the classroom. Like Ron, many of his classmates were able to orally convey their analyses of the visual verbal language of popular television at a level that seemed superior to what their comprehension scores on standardized reading tests indicated. I recall being excited by this insight, although I was not yet sure why. Several questions goaded me into reflection and action:

* Could I use popular media and technology as a springboard
   to help my students develop their print literacy?

* Would using popular media help to create a learning
   environment that invited and enabled students
   – regardless of their traditional literacy skills –
   to participate equally in the education experience?

* How might I find evidence of the value
   of using popular media with these students?

* What would popular media and media technology
   offer me in the way of methods and approaches
   to improve my teaching?

* Would teaching and studying about media
   rekindle my enthusiasm for teaching?

Schooling's Narrow View of Literacy

In light of what I learned during my Master's thesis, I became troubled by schooling's taken-for-granted narrow notion of literacy linked exclusively to decoding and encoding paper-based print texts. I was aggravated that literacy teaching in schools did not include the use of the visual language of film, television, video, photographs, advertising, and other mass media, except almost exclusively educational films. It frustrated me to think that schooling ignored the kinds of literacy around popular media which students, like mine, brought to a classroom. It angered me that school success was, in part, linked to a student's literacy abilities and his/her cognitive skills, as determined on standardized reading tests, and these scores then determined his/her placement in mainstream or special education. Indeed, I became outraged that Special Education students were being denied a position in mainstream education based in part on a print-based view and understanding of literacy.

My Early Use of Media and Technology

I decided to integrate popular media and technology into my teaching. It must be kept in mind that this was the late seventies, and the use of computers was only just making its way into mainstream classes, let alone into special education learning situations. I must admit that my initial use of media and technology in the classroom was naive and crude. Initially, I used television to attend to the traditional literary analysis processes of identifying plot, setting, character and theme(s). In fact, my early use of television was more or less a gimmick, intended to engage and motivate the students. It worked! The students seemed to get involved in analyzing television texts in ways that they had never done with print texts.

Rather than being filled with unnaturally subdued teenagers, my classes were "noisy." The students were animated, discussing, conferring, and arguing about issues related to some aspect of the programs. Even more exciting was that getting my students to put their ideas onto paper required far less coercion. Rather than having to continually ask them to show me what they had written, they were voluntarily coming to me with questions on how to spell a word, or the best way to express an idea!

In asking the questions, they had to show me what they had already written, which they willingly did. It seemed as if they now had a message, about content within a context, that they wanted to clearly convey to an audience: me. They were using a "high interest, low vocabulary" text, i.e. a television program, and in the process they were becoming more critical of their own writing, in a very positive and pedagogically appropriate way.

Over the next couple of years, I continued to include mainstream media and production work with both Special Education students and regular students. However, I did not have a real sense of direction. I was merely reacting to my concerns, intuitions, and activities that had been successful in the past.

It was not until 1990, when I attended the *First Canadian International Media Literacy Conference* in Guelph, Ontario that I learned how I was, and could be, using media texts with some sense of coherence. At the conference, I learned from Eddie Dick of Scotland about a *Conceptual Framework for Media Education*, and from Len Masterman of England, I learned about the *Key Concepts of Media Education*. This was a turning point in my professional development as a teacher. By the beginning of 1991, my changing understanding of literacy and what I had learned about Media Education at the Guelph conference led me to propose radical changes in the ACE Program.

Introducing the ACE Program

The Alternative Career Education Program (ACE) had been an important part of Lake of Two Mountains High School in The Sir Wilfrid Laurier School Board since I implemented it in 1990. ACE is a 'stay in school' program for students who are defined as being at-risk of dropping out of the formal school system because of behavioral, learning, social, or psychological issues or problems. ACE assists these at-risk students in making a transition from the formal school system to the workplace and/or to further education such as technical or vocation programs.

Beginning in 1991, I have developed and moved the ACE Program from a fairly traditional teacher directed program to a student-centered, multi-literacy, multimedia, constructivist learning environment that is relevant, motivating, and provides and supports opportunities for at-risk students to become re-engaged and re-involved in their learning. As an alternative to traditional print dominated schooling, ACE is a teen literacy program that incorporates aural, visual, print and electronic discourse and resources across the curriculum.

The ACE English Language Arts and Media Integrated Program

ACE students, as with most learning disabled students, have difficulty with print, and often consider it a threat. It seemed to me that the official government English Language Arts Program in the 1990s offered the students and myself, nothing more than a repackaged curriculum, similar to the Special Education Programs, which I had found to be of little benefit in my earlier years of teaching. In other words: same old, same old.

In redesigning the ACE Program, I tried to provide a curriculum that was both relevant and interesting to my students. This meant including learning content about the mass media and their associated technologies. It also meant using, reading, studying, and therefore validating, popular culture texts in the classroom, as well as having students create, or write, their own media texts.

I adapted the original, print oriented English Language Arts objectives to include teaching strategies that incorporated both print and non print media sources and technologies. I based my program themes around two core topics that are at the center of the ACE Program the World of Work and Life Skills. This is illustrated in *Figure 1.*

THEORY	PRACTICAL
The World of Work	
popular culture	exploring a popular text
	multi-media advertising: television, radio, magazines
media ownership	small business operation
	print & electronic journalism
cultural environment	schools, leisure, workplace
Life Skills	
media representation	examining representations of teens, gender, minorities, family

Figure 1

The curriculum – as illustrated in *Figure 1* – enabled me to integrate English, French, Mathematics, World of Work, and Life Skills courses simultaneously while incorporating popular media and technologies. In other words, the ACE Program evolved into an interdisciplinary multi-media curriculum.

I experimented with teaching strategies that were considered to be 'alternative' in that era. Students worked in groups doing collaborative projects, which included individually oriented activities. These projects required the use of various computer and media technologies. One goal of the project was the development of student autonomy while carrying out the project. Using the inquiry approach, students were required to explore, select, organize, evaluate and reflect on information that they acquired. Furthermore, they were required to present what they learned in a variety of ways: written reports, oral presentations, videos, audio tapes, posters, photographs, etc.

Soon after implementing the program, I realized that a timetable of fifty-minute periods was not suited to the integrated the curriculum that I had developed. Therefore, in late October 1992, I eliminated the rigid, rotating class timetable used in the rest of the school. Because ACE is a self-contained program, in a separate wing of the school, the Principal allowed that this timetable change would not disrupt the school. Since I was teaching the Special Education students that many mainstream teachers did not want in their classes, the teaching staff and the administration tolerated my changes, often viewed as teaching eccentricities.

To get a sense of the ACE Students' impressions of the change in their schedule: upon returning from Christmas holidays, I told the students that we were going to return to the original fifty-minute period timetable. Their reactions of annoyance, grumbling, displeasure, and petulance – through both verbal and body language – was what I had hoped to see and hear. There was a chorus of:

"Why do you want to change it? We like the longer times".
"Just when we get into something, you make us stop!"

Naturally, I backed off re-implementing the fifty-minute class periods, which I had no intention of changing. This reinforced the students' perception and understanding that they had some control over how and when they learned, which in turn made them feel more engaged and responsible for their own learning. Remember that this was happening in 1992-1993, almost twenty years before this kind of language – 'engaged' and 'responsible for their own learning' – was included in most curriculum designs. This was my first indication that at-risk students – and, I am convinced, most students – function more enthusiastically in a less fragmented, more holistic, and flexible learning schedule.

CHAPTER ONE
Inclusion or Exclusion

At-Risk Students

If I have learned anything over the last thirty plus years of teaching, it is that defining and characterizing students as 'at-risk' is problematic, and perhaps dangerous. My understanding of the descriptions and categories that these students have been placed into has shifted constantly during my teaching career.

When I first started teaching in 1977, the term used for my students was 'special education', which soon changed to 'exceptional children', then to 'high-risk', and now to 'at-risk' students. Some students were also given specific labels, such as 'emotionally and behaviorally disturbed'. My argument is not with the labels, but with the ambiguities created by these labels. The ambiguities are not a recent phenomenon, but rather are founded in the historical split between education and society. Before describing my image of the ACE students, I think it is important to provide a brief background into the origins of the historical and stereotypical image of at-risk students.

The Historical Image of At-Risk Students

Many of education's routines are founded in history, beginning in England during the reign of Henry VIII. At the age of four, children were sent to schools to become literate, so that they could learn "the word of God". Postman (1982) writes in *The Disappearance of Childhood*, "Where literacy was valued highly and persistently, there were schools and where there were schools, the concept of childhood developed rapidly" (p. 39). Unfortunately, for many children, schooling was something "unnatural", and consequently they resisted its restrictive measures.

Beginning in the middle ages, education has, with the best of intentions, operated on a system of inclusion and exclusion. Those included go on to higher levels of education; those excluded do not. This scenario seems simple enough; and yet, as Ivor Goodson reminds us in his book *School, Subjects and Curriculum Change* (1987), the idea of a "classroom" is a response to an early concept of social "class".

In the Nineteenth century, students' ability – and therefore their status within both the educational system and society – was predetermined to a degree by their social class. Upper class children were expected to go on to university. Lower class children were prepared for the world of work. This does not mean that lower class children did not have instruction in the finer points of society. Standardized English and writing invitation cards, which on the surface seems like an inappropriate task for children from poor neighborhoods, were part of the curriculum for these children.

The Stereotypical Image of At-Risk Students

In November 1990, I was given the task of following up on special education students who had been integrated into mainstream classes. On one particular day, I asked Mr. L how John was doing in his math class. (John had been integrated into a regular math class at the end of term 1). The conversation went something like this:

> **Me**: So how's John doing?
> **Mr. L**: Is John from Special Ed.?
> **Me**: Yeah, why? Is there a problem?
> **Mr. L.**: I'm not sure.
> **Me**: What's wrong?
> **Mr. L**: Well he's doing o.k, he's cooperating and
> . . . but, is he on medication or taking dope?
> **Me**: Not that I know of, why? What's he doing?
> **Mr. L.**: Nothing's wrong. I just didn't know he was from
> Special Ed, and I figured if he's doing well,
> then he must be on medication.

I include this conversation not as a critique of teachers, but rather as an example of how the stereotyping of students who are – or were – placed in non mainstreamed classes has continued. My stereotypical image of low-achieving students, constructed over the last thirty-one years, is of one who:

* Has difficulty with classmates
* Is disruptive and uncooperative
* Has a short attention span
* Is activity oriented
* lacks higher reasoning skills
* Is unable to work with abstract concepts
* Is afraid to take risks
* Is not goal oriented

During the 1960s, students who came from visible minority groups, single parent families, and/or low income families were considered socio-culturally deprived, lacked parental support, and consequently did poorly in school. It was assumed that socio-culturally deprived students were unable to attain basic skills, the prerequisites for higher order skills, and therefore could not meet hierarchical curriculum standards (Means, Chelemer and Knapp, 1991). Thus, they tended to drop out of school earlier than most other students.

Further studies by Means, Chelemer, and Knapp (1991) have found that students experiencing difficulty attaining basic skills in school, include those who have one or more of the following characteristics:

* Mostly males
* History of family related problems
* Substance abuse
* Early pregnancies
* Single parent families
* Poorly educated mothers
* Limited ability in the English language.

Typically, such students were, and are considered today, to display one or more of the following behaviors:

* Do not participate in and/or identify with their school
* Disciplinary problems
* High rate of truancy
* Impulsive behaviors
* Poor peer relationships
* Low self esteem
* emotional problems
* Communicate most often through actions, rather than words
* Externally oriented rather than introspective
* Content oriented rather than form centered

Perhaps the most misleading description of students alternatively schooled comes from *The Official Politically Correct Dictionary and Handbook* (Beard and Cerf, 1993). Students, who are placed outside of mainstream education are considered "uneducated; illiterate" (p. 6).

A 1992 Federal study reported in one of Canada's newspapers counters the stereotypical notion that low achievers are the most at-risk of dropping out of school. According to the report, 77% of 18 to 20 year olds who had dropped out of school had passing grades. Thirty seven percent had A or B averages, 40% had C's. At the opposite end, 33% of students who graduated had backgrounds that were considered high risk: low income and/or single parent families, or were themselves married with children, but had family or other influences which discouraged educational success.

You're Either Included or Excluded: You're Either In or Out

June 20, 1996 was hot and muggy. The last place I felt like being was in my high school staff room, calculating students' marks. As I thumbed through the stack of papers, I listened to some of my colleagues discussing the frustrating state of education. For many teachers, exam time is often the catalyst for the ritual of bashing the educational system, and more specifically, for commenting on students who, through their own fault (according to their teachers) have not done well during the school year and/or on the exams.

Owing to the high humidity and end of year exhaustion, I had little energy to begin a conversation with these teachers on critical pedagogy. That is, until the discussion turned toward the notion that there are those students "who are academics and go on to university, and there are those who don't go to university because they can't learn, can't remember, aren't motivated, and would benefit more from a program like ACE".

My colleagues' discussion in the staff room was not deliberately meant to be derogatory. It was how they saw their world, and the students in it. Still, the children they were focusing on were those for whom education had failed to provide an environment that invited them into the learning process. My colleagues' discussion points to an ideological conceptualization of literacy, which sees two solitudes in a high school education: one for students who have become literate, and one for those who will never become literate.

There is an old story that I have seen on many teacher staffroom bulletin boards that goes something like this:

The high school teacher blames the elementary school
teacher, because the students can't read.

The elementary school teacher blames the parents,
because the students came to school unprepared to learn.

The mother blames the father,
because he wasn't there to help prepare
the child for school and life.

The father blames the medical system,
because there was a problem at the child's birth.

The medical system blames
the gene pool that created the child.

There is certainly truth in the statements that:

* Not all children can or should go onto higher education,
* There is a need for alternative programs for some students,
* Every student has strengths and weaknesses.

Admittedly, early on in my teaching career, I followed what were then the latest educational trends, and referred to my students as low achieving, general, special education, disadvantaged, educationally deprived, exceptional, learning disabled, emotionally disturbed, at-risk, drop-outs, and, most recently, educationally challenged. Over the last thirty years, I have also taught a number of remedial programs that included: Short Vocation, Special Education, Individualized Learning, Continuous, Individualized Learning Temporary, Cooperative Education, 16+(Plus), and, of course, Alternative Education. Now I use the terms "at-risk students" and "alternative program".

In fact, I welcome students' individual abilities. However, at the risk of sounding like an evangelical teacher, I appreciate that my students can learn, remember, and be motivated to succeed in school. Consequently, I bristle when my students, and others like them, are described in ways that position them on the lower end fringes of education. I am often told by colleagues that students who are "having trouble", the code phrase for disruptive behavior, "would be better off in the ACE Program", which demonstrates the assumption that alternative programs such as ACE are dumping grounds for those who are either not succeeding in, or are being disruptive in mainstream classes.

Perhaps *The Education Indicators for the Elementary and Secondary Levels* (Ministere de l'education: Direction des etudes economiques et demographiques, 1993) best illustrates the point I have made here regarding inclusionary and exclusionary schooling. The document states (the italics are mine):

Some students who are *intellectually challenged* leave secondary school *without a diploma after having attended school until 21 years of age.* Other students enrolled in "continuous individualized path for learning" enter a life skills or work skills program at the age of 16. The latter students may obtain an Attestation of Skills issued by the school board. *Although this certificate recognizes a certain level of achievement, it is not formally issued by the Ministere, nor is it equivalent to a diploma awarded by the Ministere* (p. 42).

While the report goes on to say that "*Strictly speaking, students described above cannot be considered drop outs*" (p. 42), it does state that 32.2 per cent of "early school leavers", who are students eligible for high school graduation, dropped out of school in the school year 1991-1992. This was an increase from 27 percent in the mid 1980s. The report suggests that the increase was due to *intellectually challenged students* leaving school without a diploma. Stricter graduation requirements, and the move to transfer students over the age of eighteen to the adult education sector were the triggers.

My Image of At-Risk Students: The ACE Students

Demographically, some ACE students do fit many of the behavioral, social, economic and family characteristics, of at-risk students described earlier by Means, Chelemer, and Knapp (1991). However, for most students, the opposite is true. In fact, characterizing the "average" ACE student is as problematic as defining at-risk students.

The ACE students vary in age from sixteen to nineteen. Most are English speaking mother tongue, some are French mother tongue, most of them are bilingual, speaking both English and French. They are physically and socially indistinguishable from typical high school students. They aspire to be successful academically and vocationally, and most are actually quite capable learners.

Furthermore, while there are some ACE students who display negative behaviors and attitudes associated with the stereotypical idea of at-risk students, ACE students are capable of cooperative learning. They want to succeed. They want to learn. They do not want to drop out of school. They are naturally curious. They are adaptable to new situations. They are capable of higher level thinking. Indeed, they are not unlike the typical Lake of Two Mountains High School (LTMHS) "regular students".

Still, there are some attributes which only ACE students share:

* They have previously enrolled in regular, special education, or Individual Paths for Learning (IPL) classes.

* Their average reading levels are between grade five and grade seven, placing them well below grade nine, the norm for students aged sixteen years.

* There are some ACE students who are reading and writing at the pre high school level.

* They have been denied access to a high school diploma within the structures as they now exist in Quebec high schools, because they have very few high school credits, and some have none.

* They cannot complete the required courses in the allotted amount of time, using approaches and methods of evaluation used in mainstream classes. Indeed, some never will attain this measure of success.

* The results of their negative experiences in school and at home have left many students "turned off" of schooling.

Here are comments taken from ACE students' journals that highlight some of the above characteristics. They were written in response to a general class discussion about schooling, and how they felt about it:

"Even though I haven't dropped out, I have thought about it quite a bit. I did and am going through difficult times. These problems, either family related or school related doesn't make a difference. I messed up my high school years. I have been put back for the past two years."

"Yes, I have thought of dropping out. I was doing nothing in my classes. I would walk in my sleep."

"The thing is that you blame yourself and also the process is   very hard and long one and that really hurts".

Some ACE students have dropped out of school, returning discouraged at being unable to find employment. Asked why she wanted to enter the ACE Program, J.L wrote:

"To learn and when your finished school you take your degree and you try to find a job and most times you find one but now with the economy falling in Quebec its harder to find a job. There's a lot of people unemployed in this province and if there's a lot of people out of work well the chances of me finding a job is very slim."

Another student wrote:

"I was put in the ACE Program because the traditional school was not working for me. The traditional school was too fast for me i needed some kind of program that would not be so fast and it could help me do up some of my potential. I was thinking i was not getting any younger and i needed some kind of work experience because i knew that i couldn't get my diploma as fast as the regular students. ACE seemed like my best chances."

English Language Arts, Media Literacy and Literacy Curriculum in the ACE Program

In designing the English Language Arts curriculum for the ACE students, I saw connections between the English Language Arts Program I was teaching and what I learned about Media Education at the Guelph Conference, from media colleagues and books on the subject.

My thinking is that English Language Arts Education and Media Education both have Literacy as their primary goal, which accounts for the reason that English Language Arts teachers are primarily the ones teaching Media Education, and why the pioneering theorists in Media Education are mostly former English teachers. Upon closer examination, it is easy to see the connections between English Language Arts Education and Media Education. As you will see later on, I have exploited these connections to describe my students' literate behaviors. For now, literate behavior can be considered "a conscious use of new or expanding repertoires as readers and writers" (Emery, Anderson, Rother, Tiseo, Mitchell, & Brandeis, 1995). While considerable progress has been made in the development and implementation of Media Education Curricula and materials, very little has been written about the adequacy of the theory to describe the literate behavior of students or the effectiveness of the curricula in eliciting it.

In 1988, UNESCO stated that in regards to literacy, there was a lack of systematic studies on the use of media in this area, which prompted me to consider what kinds of literate behaviors ACE students demonstrated following the Media Education Curriculum I had developed. And following this, how are these kinds of literate behaviors consistent with and/or are inconsistent with formal schoolings' notion of literacy? At the same time, I was also interested in the following:

* What aspects of the Media Education Curriculum contributed to the ACE student learning?

* What kinds of knowledge do ACE students bring to bear as producers and consumers of media following participation in a Media Education Curriculum?

* Does my Media Education Curriculum assist ACE students' understanding of traditional print texts?

* What kind of teaching approaches and principles seem to be appropriate?

Other media educators explored the impact of Media Education on students' knowledge of media. For instance, McMahon and Quin's (1992) study attempted to investigate whether Australian curricula in Media Literacy provided students with the knowledge of the media specified in the curricula. This large scale study was conducted with "regular stream" elementary and secondary students, and relied on a pen and paper test requiring the students to analyse a sitcom and three different print advertisements. McMahon and Quin found the pen and paper method of data collection inadequate in helping them determine the extent to which the Australian Media Literacy curricula enabled students to demonstrate their understanding of media texts (here media texts are meant to be print and audio visual).

Buckingham and Sefton Green (1994) have conducted an in-depth analysis of students' production, analysis and use of media in a large secondary school in North London. The focus of the study was on the relationships between young people's involvement in popular culture outside of school, and their experiences of Media Education within a formal school curriculum. While much could be inferred from the descriptions of the students' work, the study did not explicitly address their literate behavior.

CHAPTER TWO
Media Education,
Media Studies, and Media Literacy

The British publication *Media Education in Britain: An Outline* (1989) defined Media Education as any progressive development of critical understanding that seeks to extend pupils' knowledge of the media, and to develop their analytical and creative skills through critical and practical work (p. 2). This definition includes television, film, radio, books and all the new media.

Over the last decade, the terms Media Education, Media Studies, and Media Literacy have been used almost interchangeably by media educators in North America, Britain, and Australia. The following distinctions have been adapted from Buckingham (1993b), Lusted (1991), Masterman (1985), *Media Education in Britain: An Outline* (1989), Moore (1991), Silverblatt (1995), and Worsnop (1994):

Media Education includes:

* Using media across the curriculum application
* Topic within another subject
* Develops critical understanding of media
  through analytical and practical work
* Includes teaching about the forms, conventions,
  and technologies
* Includes teaching about media institutions,
  and their social, political and cultural roles
* Places emphasis upon students' experience of the media
  and their relevance to their own lives;
* Themes and project work;
* Borrows from audio visual literacy
  and English Language Arts;
* North American influence.

Media Studies on the other hand includes:

* Cross media application;
* Theoretical application of the media;
* Conceptual framework;
* Incorporates analysis of a message delivered by the media and the techniques used to create that message;
* Borrows from communication, film and cultural studies;
* British, Australian, and European influence.

Media Literacy builds on the following outcomes of Media Education and Media Studies:

* An awareness of the impact of media on the individual and society;
* An understanding of the process of mass communication;
* The ability to analyse and discuss media messages;
* An awareness of media context as a text that provides recognition of culture;
* Production and analysis skills;
* traditional and non traditional literacy skills;
* an enriched enjoyment, understanding and appreciation of media content.

The definition of Media Literacy according to the *Ontario Department of Education Resource Guide: Intermediate and Senior Divisions* (Ministry of Education, Ontario, 1989) is:

Media Literacy is concerned with helping students develop an informed and critical understanding of the nature of the mass media, the techniques used by them, and the impact of these techniques. More specifically, it is education that aims to increase students' understanding and enjoyment of how the media work, how they produce meaning, how they are organised, and how they construct reality. Media Literacy also aims to provide students with the ability to create media products (pp. 6-7).

In *Media Literacy: A Report of the National Leadership Conference on Media Literacy*, a basic definition of Media Literacy is stated as:

> The ability of a citizen to access, analyze, and produce information for specific outcomes (Aufderheide, 1993, p. V).

Teaching Through and About the Media: The Difference

There has also been confusion about teaching *through* media and teaching *about* media. Duncan (1993) states that teaching *through* the media, while concerned with the language of media, primarily focuses on using media as a vehicle to initiate discussion, or as a motivator for English Language Arts classes. In other words, in teaching through the media, teachers use the media as a delivery system for subject content. No attempt to examine the delivery system itself is made.

In teaching *about* the media, the delivery system is also examined. Further, teaching about the media stems from the notion that media shape the world in which we live, and therefore it is becoming increasingly important for students to understand the infrastructures of society. Media Education explores the media within a socio-political framework through analysis and production. This includes preparing students to understand the production and dissemination of information, the growth of media industry, the development of commercially-based media, the role of advertising, and audience negotiation of print and non print text.

In 1972, a meeting of Member Organizations, UNESCO, defined Media Education as:

> The study, learning and teaching of, and about the modern media of communication and expression as a specific and autonomous area of knowledge within educational theory and practice, distinct from their own use as aids for teaching and learning of other areas of knowledge, such as mathematics, science and geography.

This definition describes the relationship between Media Education and aspects of communication studies, literary criticism, journalism, social science, and technology. It points out that Media Education is a means of understanding the media within various disciplines. My focus is concerned with teaching about media.

You will notice that I have decided to use the term Media Education to describe the program the ACE students were exposed, and their literate behavior indicates Media Literacy and traditional literacy.

A Postmodern Definition of Literacy

Willinsky (1991) provides a set of principles that accommodate a view of Media Education, as well as support a notion of an expanded definition of literacy. His principles are summarized as:

1. What counts in postmodern literacy is the use of language rather than the medium or technology that produces it.

2. Texts in postmodern literacy are not fixed creations but develop through collaboration and appropriation of texts that already exist.

3. Postmodern literacy embraces notions of literacy that all texts, oral, written and visual are dependent on the socio-cultural meaning of signs (i.e., semiotics).

4. Postmodern literacy broadens our concept of texts beyond the symbolic nature of language to include man made environments. In Willinsky's terms, postmodern literacy promotes reading of "arche(texture)" (p. 67).

5. By "finding a place for one's story and a form to make it stick" (p. 60), we are able to make meaning of the world.

6. Postmodern literacy operates on a series of distinctions between production of meaning, publication, originality, economic and moral obligations.

7. Postmodern literacy acknowledges the contribution of mainstream popular culture forms as sites for exploring the relationship between one's position in society and the socio-political ideologies in society.

8. Postmodern literacy acknowledges oppositional texts found in popular culture forms, and encourages the reading and writing of alternative texts.

9. Postmodern literacy recognizes the juxtaposition of sign systems, specifically art and economics found in advertising.

10. Postmodern literacy endorses the theoretical and production aspects of Media Studies in order to help students demystify media texts.

11. Postmodern literacy acknowledges that it is not the panacea for dealing with all the social and ideological issues in the world. Nor does postmodern literacy claim to be the answer to assist those who do not meet the demands of traditional schooling.

12. Postmodern literacy is critical literacy that, through the use of language, promotes public consciousness of social, cultural, and economic ideologies.

Willinsky's description of postmodern literacy represents the changes in conceptualisations of literacy that have occurred recently in the evolution of English Language Arts Education. The evolution I am referring to has taken place over the last century.

CHAPTER THREE
Evolving Notions of Literacy in English Studies

The Harvard influence

The relationship between English teaching and the communication media has a long history. Early notions of English Teaching in North American schools ranged from instructing students to read great authors as a means to teach composition (Applebee, 1974) to reading the Bible and using literature to improve morality (Gere, 1992; Shayer, 1972). During the late nineteenth century, English teaching in North America was concerned with teaching literature. Applebee (1974) cites the example of entrance requirements for Harvard University of 1873-74, which set the standard for all tertiary education in the United States, as well as the rest of North America. Candidates were required to "write a short English composition, correct in spelling, punctuation, grammar, and expression, the subject to be taken from such works of standard authors as well, as shall be announced from time to time" (Harvard University, 1873, in Applebee, 1974, p. 30). In 1899, university entrance requirements specified that high school students be exposed to "classics" such as *Ivanhoe, Silas Marner, Idylls of the King, A Tale of Two Cities*, and *Julius Caesar.* Shayer (1972) refers to the "classical fallacy" of English teaching that lasted until the nineteen thirties:

Its origins lie in the uneasy transition from the almost exclusive study of the classics as the one true literary discipline to the acceptance of English at the turn of the century, with the belief that despite its pale substitute nature, it (English) could be respectable, providing (and only providing) that it was treated classically. While it was regarded by many as an upstart, its advocates were anxious to prove its integrity by distorting its real nature, a somewhat ironic capitulation when one considers that the classical studies themselves were exclusively biased on the grammatical linguistic side at the time. The situation was not helped by the fact that the early teacher of English (certainly in the secondary school) was more likely than not a converted classicist and prone to fall back upon the methods of the Classical curriculum in which he had been trained (p. 6).

The real objective of early English teaching was to have a student write grammatically correct prose composition. Literature was considered purely as a subject matter for composition, the imitation of models, and mastering of a set of rules. There was no attempt to involve the knowledge or experience that a student brought to the learning. Shayer (1972) states:

> What is so false in such an approach is the assumption that writing in one's own language is purely a matter of externals, the confronting of a mental obstacle course that the writer will best get through if he keeps his personal feelings in abeyance (p. 7).

The emphasis was on reading classical texts as models of good composition, in order to imitate, copy, or reproduce them. Shayer again notes that:

> Composition becomes the expansion of predetermined notes, the teacher's or the textbook writer's, not the child's, and the final mark awarded will depend as much on the pupil's ability to keep to the straight and narrow of the imposed framework as on spelling, punctuation and handwriting (p. 11). The almost exclusive focus on literature, which stemmed from the requirements for entrance into university, drove secondary school curricula.

As the nineteenth century came to a close, psychologists interested in learning and pedagogy argued against the idea that adult models of English should be imposed on children. They developed notions of instruction based on the individual characteristics of a learner.

At the forefront of such thinking were G. Stanley Hall and John Dewey. Hall and Mansfield (1886) stressed the need for curriculum to reflect the stages of a child's development. He argued that texts be selected according to students' reading ability and their psychological development. The texts should be selected on the basis of whether they would be of interest to students, rather than purely on their literary merit.

Further, Hall's interest in the psychological development of a child also included a child's moral development. Texts,such as the Bible were to be studied for the values they expressed, as well as for their content. His thinking in this area proved to be significant since it essentially asked students to respond to the meaning of a text. Hall influenced not only which texts should be chosen, but also influenced a shift in English instruction based on the characteristics of a child (Applebee, 1974).

The Progressive Movement

Hall's writing influenced the thinking of John Dewey, who in 1889 emphasised the relationships between a child, his/her community, and school. Dewey was concerned with a child's social awareness of society, and the importance of imaginative experience (Shayer, 1972). According to Applebee (1974), Dewey's ideas mitigated the influences of the university on high school curricula. Dewey rejected the belief that literature and history were the sole determinants of culture.

Dewey also disputed the idea of a cultural elite in education. He envisioned a democratising of the educational system, in which a child grew within a social environment stressing cooperation and group work. That is, Dewey made the connection between a child centered notion of English teaching and literacy. Dewey's work is important for Media Education, since it advocates a hands on experiential, inquiry based approach to learning.

The Committee Of Ten

The progressive movement posed a serious challenge to the Harvard model of literacy, and its concomitant approach to English teaching regarding not only which texts should be studied in secondary schools, but also the teaching approaches that were appropriate.

The number of texts used in secondary school English classes further complicated the confusion among teachers about how to incorporate the Harvard and Progressive style of English teaching. Literary texts for secondary schools varied from university to university. Each university decided which texts they would use to examine secondary students for university entrance. Problems such as this, along with the variations in university entrance requirements in other areas of the secondary curriculum, prompted The National Education Council of the United States to form a Committee of Ten in 1892 to deal with the difficulties (Applebee, 1974). Half of the Committee of Ten members came from secondary schools, while the other half were from universities.

The Committee of Ten organised a series of nine conferences, each based on a different area of the curriculum, including one for English. Each conference organised their own commissions, and were required to report their findings about how to deal with the difficulties in entrance requirements to the main body of the Committee of Ten.

The commission charged with dealing with English teaching reported that the purpose of English is to:

1. Enable the pupil to understand the expressed thoughts of others and to give expression to thoughts of his own.

2. To cultivate a taste for reading, to give the pupil some acquaintance with good literature, and to furnish him with the means of extending that acquaintance
(Applebee, 1974, p. 33).

The Committee of Ten's report of 1894 was significant in establishing English as a valid subject. It gave full recognition to English teaching by recommending that it be taught to all students at the four levels of secondary school. Also, it placed literature at the center of the English Program, suggesting that by the first year of secondary school, students should be exposed to poetry and narrative.

However, the report's emphasis on literature resulted in a uniform list of classical texts, as well as a large number of annotated series, which were to be used for university entrance requirements. The establishment of a uniform canon of classical texts resulted in a backlash among many English teachers. It raised the question as to what and who determines a classical text. The other concern was who should be determining university requirements, the secondary schools or the universities.

Indeed, while the final report of the Committee of Ten, and the subsequent National Conference on Uniform Entrance Requirements entrenched English in the secondary school curriculum, its conception of English was counter to the progressive notions of Dewey, since it ignored the interest and ability of a child.

Early Twentieth Century Developments: The Introduction of Popular Texts

The Committee of Ten's approach to literature, which focused on the rhetoric, narration, description, and exposition of a uniform list of classical texts (Applebee, 1974, p. 49) invoked resistance by secondary school English teachers. They rejected the idea that they had no input in how to prepare students for university entrance. The dissatisfaction led to the formation of the National Council of Teachers of English (NCTE) in 1911.

While the NCTE maintained that there needed to be an established level of English competency, it realized that not all students were bound for university, and therefore the curriculum should be adapted to accommodate those students as well. The NCTE helped to democratise English teaching. It addressed the needs of children from various backgrounds by including books in the list of classical texts approved by the Committee of Ten which could be read at home. It also contributed by supporting and sustaining the expansion of school libraries to include all types of books, and not just "classical" texts.

The 1914 *Handbook of Suggestions* (cited in Shayer, 1972) advocated that junior classes should include fairy tales, legends and myths, animal stories, adventures, and children experiences. The *Handbook* also urged that children should be freed from the stress of making mistakes in their writing; teachers should help students to be become autonomous in finding their own errors (Shayer, 1972).

In 1916, the actions of the NCTE pressured the National Conference on Uniform Entrance Requirements to offer secondary schools the option of providing students with a "restrictive" examination based on the uniform list, or a "comprehensive" examination, which tested a student's comprehension and appreciation of a variety of different literature. In other words, control of preparation for university entrance exams was slowly relinquished to the level of the secondary school. By 1931 the uniform list was discarded (Applebee, 1974).

The slow transition at the end of the nineteenth century and beginning of the twentieth century to accommodate the perceived interests of the students prompted teachers to utilize modern writings that appealed to the students in order to motivate them. This was especially true for those students not bound for post secondary education. In early twentieth century English classrooms, teachers tolerated newspapers, magazines, and comics as means by which they might assist lower class children to develop an interest in common mainstream texts and transfer it to classical literature (Applebee, 1974). "Modern texts" were used to demonstrate to students the advantages of higher levels of culture (i.e., classical canons of literature) over lower culture (i.e., mass media texts).

Practical Literacy

The period immediately preceding, during, and following the First World War saw a movement towards a view of English teaching, which emphasized producing good citizens (Gere, 1992). Educators believed that if the economy of the 1920s was to improve, it would require a population that was literate enough to acquire employment. Since it was expected that all adults were to be gainfully employed, the notion was that being able to read and write was a basic skill, not just for those destined for post secondary education. With this in mind, there was an attempt to improve the communication skills and socially useful skills of lower class students. However, many of the skills that were taught (such as writing invitations and thank you notes) were foreign to lower class citizens.

Two levels of literacy were thus developing: a lower level, and a higher level. The lower level of literacy included basic skills of reading and writing for those who are not bound for post secondary education, but who could acquire employment and maintain the economy of society. The implication was that some students were less capable of higher level reasoning, and therefore less capable of analysis of classical literature and proper composition. The higher level of literacy was for the academic intellectual, bound for post secondary education, and who could direct the political, social, and economic structures. In other words, notions of literacy during the 1920s, 30s, and 40s were based on a socio-cultural hierarchy made up of a work force who could maintain the economic base of society ,and an academic force who could manage the socio-political affairs of the population. This notion existed well into the 50s. For instance, Bantock (1952) argues against progressive student centered notions of education such as that advocated by Dewey. He commented that the majority of students had no real place in the traditional grammar school, since they lacked the mental abilities and discipline.

UNESCO's Definition of Literacy

Following World War II, English curricula continued to reflect practical and academic emphases and their concomitant views of literacy. Again, there were swings of the pendulum from progressive pedagogical approaches and the selection of texts that reflected students' life experiences, and interest to more traditional teacher centered pedagogy and the selection of classical texts (Applebee, 1974).

The preceding descriptions of early notions of literacy have focused on events in North America, particularly the United States. From an examination of the history of Media Education, similar notions appear to have been held in Britain (see for example, Leavis and Thompson, 1933).

In the 1950s, the newly formed UNESCO undertook to define literacy. The definition reflected, to some extent, the stance of the key member nations, largely English speaking, incorporating the "practical" conceptualisation of literacy. In 1951, for example, the organization considered that, "a person is literate who can, with understanding, both read and write a short, simple statement on his everyday life" (cited in Department of Education and Science, 1975). This definition reflects a minimal requirement of literacy that is characteristic of a lower level of literacy described earlier. Five years later, UNESCO modified their definition of literacy to "a person is literate when he has acquired the essential knowledge and skills which enable him to engage in all those activities in which literacy is required for effective functioning in his group and community" (Gray, 1956, p. 21).

This definition moves beyond linking literacy with the work place. It acknowledges the relationship of literacy to public as well as economic contexts.

UNESCO's definition of literacy, which included a socio-political context, was overshadowed with the launching of Sputnik in 1957 by the Soviet Union. The Western world became concerned that it was falling behind in the pursuit of education excellence which was linked to levels of literacy. The thinking was, and still is, that if you raise the levels of literacy, from lower levels to higher levels, then academic levels are also raised. This notion resulted in an even further division between a lower and a higher level of literacy. In 1962, UNESCO clarified functional literacy even further:

> Literacy is the possession by an individual of the essential knowledge and skills which enable him to engage in all those activities required for effective functioning in his group and community and whose attainments in reading, writing and arithmetic make it possible for him to use these skills toward his own and the community's development (UNESCO, 1962).

English Teaching in The 1960s

English teaching during the 1950s and into the early 1960s emphasized language, literature, and composition (Gere, 1992). For the most part, the social and cultural aspects of a child were ignored, just as they had been at the beginning of the century. In education, a child's background – including their everyday language – was considered an irritant well into the 1960s and 70s. Students were expected to conform to a Standard of English which enabled them to properly carry on their daily affairs in writing and speech, and which reflected an educated individual. In other words, people at higher levels of literacy should use Standard English. Those who did not use Standard English were considered illiterate, and anomalies who had to be righted. It was commonly held that Standard English was to be acquired by some students in school, and never by others, such as special education students.

Unfortunately, during the 1960s, cultural and social differences, such as race and place of origin, were seen as partially responsible for differences in language ability. Remedial programs were designed to assist students with language difficulties. Until the early 1970s, English teaching ignored the language gains many children made before coming to school.

1970s English Teaching
and The Dartmouth Conference

The late 1960s and early 70s were years of tremendous tension and change in schooling, as well as in society. Social and political unrest, which challenged traditional beliefs and values, had its affect on the teaching of English in North America and Britain. Teachers began to consider new approaches to the teaching of English, such as classroom drama, small group discussion, and about incorporating themes on topics that would be relevant to students (Applebee, 1977).

The social and educational concerns led to a dialog about the teaching of English. In 1966, fifty elementary, secondary, and university educators from England, the United States, and a single representative from Canada, met at Dartmouth College in New Hampshire at the Anglo American Seminar on the Teaching of English. The objective of the conference was to explore international opinions about what was right and wrong with how English was being taught, particularly in elementary and secondary schools. Each of the Dartmouth participants came to the conference with views about the nature of English, and how it should be taught in schools.

Literacy prior to the Dartmouth Conference was based on the previously discussed notions of an elitist, higher level of literacy for students bound for post secondary school, and a purely, functional lower level of literacy for those who were bound to enter directly into the work force. These models of literacy were handed down to schools. In other words, students who fit into the higher level of literacy model were part of a literate world. This elitist form of literacy was prevalent at the high school and elementary school level.

Dixon (1969) summarizes the main points of agreement about language education developed at the Dartmouth Conference. These are:

1. Language is learned bydoing, not by practice exercises.

2. Students must share life experiences through dialog, monologue, talk, literature, drama, and writing.

3. Using shared experience, students construct their own understanding of reality.

4. Students learn how to write well as they begin to understand the role of the writing process in message design.

5. The role of a teacher is to navigate a student through the writing process.

6. Students may also seek assistance in the writing process from their classmates.

7. Students develop new insights through active participation with the symbolic nature of language.

8. Children learn language prior to coming to school from parents, family, and their neighbourhoods.

9. Language use and development prior to coming to school is limited by the degree of social interaction experienced by a child.

10. The teaching of English begins with and builds upon the recognition of a child's unique language background and experience.

11. The role of English teaching is to help a student move successfully and confidently from the spoken to the written, from dialect to standard and from dialog to monologue

(Dixon, 1969).

The main points of the Dartmouth Conference have several important implications for an expanded notion of literacy. For the first time in the development of English teaching, the importance of student knowledge and use of language prior to coming to school were acknowledged. Second, participants at Dartmouth generally agreed that no one way of teaching English exists, since not one child's language development is the same (Muller, 1967, p. 53). Third, teachers at Dartmouth recognized the role of language in the everyday experiences of a child, and that meaningful writing occurs when a student can negotiate and share his or her own experiences. That is, they conceived of literacy as an active process that involves the everyday experiences of students. The Dartmouth Conference also marked a change in the use of the term English teaching to Language Arts education. Finally, and most significant, the main points of the Dartmouth Conference, previously outlined, illustrate that schooling needed to provide more opportunities for students to use language for their own purposes, in different contexts according to different functions.

James Britton: The Functions of Language

Prior to Dartmouth, the language that students used with family and in the community, its purposes, and its context were of little importance. The only form of language that was of concern to teachers was Standard English. Gere and Smith (1979) describe the myths which constitute notions of Standard English:

1. Standard English is the kind of language which people should use for all occasions. Standard means most serviceable and negotiable and therefore most correct.

2. Standard English is a clearly definable set of correct pronunciations, grammatical structures, and word choices. It is standard because it represents the widest usage and because it has been refined to be the most versatile and acceptable form of English.

3. Standard English is necessary for success in school and therefore in employment. One of the principal reasons for having schools is to equip young people with the skills necessary to improve their chances of social and financial rewards. Conformity to certain ways of using language obviously underlies several of those skills.

4. Standard English is the best version of English for the expression of logical and abstract thought. Because all of the great English and American writers use this form of English and because much of the business of our society is conducted with this form, it must be the form best suited to the expression of precise and sophisticated thought (p. 8).

These notions of a singular, proper Standard English changed after Dartmouth. A major contributor to this shift was James Britton (1975). Britton examined the writing development of children between the ages of eleven and eighteen. His research focused on "the demands that different tasks make upon the writer [i.e., functions] and the writer's expectations with regard to the reader usually the teacher [i.e., audience]" (p. 10).

Participants and Spectators

Britton's concept of participant and spectator provides a framework that focuses on the purposes of why a person writes, and includes how language is used to represent our experiences (p. 79). According to Britton, we understand our world by being both a participant and a spectator. As participants, we are required to evaluate experiences so that we may be able to act in one way or another. Our evaluations of the experiences act as triggers for action. For a participant, content is more significant than the form and the emotional or affective nature of language.

A spectator, on the other hand, is afforded the luxury of making value judgments without necessarily having to act upon those judgments. A writer, as a spectator, understands the world by evaluating his/her emotional responses to experiences. Language for a spectator becomes a means through which to reflect and express an understanding of the world. Britton stresses that a child must be able to operate in the role of spectator, using the knowledge of language that he has built before coming to school, as well as in school as a participant. Literacy that includes the concept of participants and spectators is something that we develop as generators and interpreters of language. The differences between participant and spectator provide a framework for the functions of written language.

The Functions of Language: The Expressive Function

For Britton, the expressive use of language is the most important function of language. He describes expressive language both in terms of spoken and written. Expressive language that is spoken includes expressions of emotions, expressions of inner thoughts, expressions of emotional needs, and expressions of moods. Expressive language in written form includes thinking aloud on paper, journal writing, letter writing to a friend, writing to more than one audience who share common values and experiences (Britton, 1975). Expressive language fulfils the basic needs of individuals to use language in order to articulate their own world to themselves and to others. Expressive language is affective in nature, since the author spontaneously includes his /her own emotional responses to a situation. Britton argues that teachers should be providing more opportunities for students to use expressive language. He also stresses that early writing in schools must begin with expressive language so that children are able to move into what he refers to as the transactional and poetic functions of language.

Transactional and Poetic Functions

Participants use the transactional function of language to inform, persuade and advise. The function of transactional language is to fulfill an outcome. The form of the transactional language is organised so that the writer needs only to make sure that a reader is able to make connections about what is expected. In other words, transactional language is characterised by its practicality. Examples of the transactional function are: business reports, recording of information, and radio or television scripts.

On the other hand, spectators use poetic language to recreate experience to entertain. That is, poetic language serves a primary function to give pleasure to an author and an audience. As a result, form and context are essential in the poetic function of language if a reader is to understand and appreciate meaning.

Britton notes that expressive language is always at play in both transactional and poetic functions. Expressive language operates within the transactional function when the reader is coerced into performing or responding to a task. Expressive language moves into the poetic function when a reader is asked to make meaning of experience.

Audience and Schooling

The ability to modify one's writing for different functions acknowledges the notion of audience. Britton observes that writing for an audience is a difficult concept for novice writers, since it involves understanding how to address the needs of different audiences in specific contexts. Writing is also difficult for beginning writers, since they must become what Britton refers to as, "performers of a social act in the arena of context, or situation" (p. 60). His analogy implies that writing for an audience, whom one may or may not know, moves beyond writing for the self (i.e., expressive language) and into a social relationship between a writer and a reader (i.e., transactional or poetic language). A writer must always keep in mind who they are writing for, the purpose of the writing and under what circumstances their writing will be read (i.e., the function and context).

While Britton acknowledges the importance of student understanding of the role of audience in the development and process of writing, he also recognizes the difficulties that teaching audience presents in schools. A student sees his/her own writing development not only determined by the teacher's standards, but also the teacher's socio-cultural values. He states:

> "The messages which flow from the pupil writer to teacher audience will be affected by the extent to which they share common cultural assumptions and also by the extent to which the pupil is aware of how matters stand" (p. 63).

As a result, young writers will unfortunately often consider their own pleasure or insights as secondary (p. 6) and will write for the teacher rather than for themselves.

Britton's work is significant for Media Education, since it breaks away from the notion of singular form of Standard English as described earlier. He argues for a use of language as a valid form of communication, spoken and written to please oneself as well as for an audience, and in more than one function and context. This includes language typically used in films, television, and radio programs.

Douglas Barnes:
Classroom Language and Communication

While Britton has contributed the notion of the expressive function of language as being the base from which transactional and poetic functions develop, Barnes (1992) considers how opportunities may be generated in classrooms in order to develop children's expressive abilities. His work brings into focus the changing pedagogical practices implicit in the student centered considerations of post Dartmouth conceptualisation of the English Language Arts such as Britton's.

In his study of third year classes in eleven schools, Barnes asked teachers to respond to the following questions:

1. Why they set written work,
2. What they kept in mind when they set it,
3. What they did in marking pupils' writings, and
4. What uses, if any, they made of it after marking (p. 139).

From their responses, he was able to identify what he refers to as transmission and interpretation views of teaching.

In the transmission view of teaching, student writing is a means to an end product. Writing is an exercise through which teachers correct errors in content or grammar. Marking is used for assessment purposes only. The resulting tendency is that teachers point out problems rather than progress. The transmission teacher's objective is to provide students with knowledge, which can then be tested. This type of teaching produces what Barnes refers to as school knowledge.

School knowledge is presented by the teacher as knowledge that requires that students have enough of an understanding that will enable them to correctly fulfill examination questions. It therefore has no reference points from which students can relate the information to their own experiences (i.e., understandings and values). School knowledge is never the property of students. It is knowledge hidden between pages of books, or in a teacher's mind. Barnes argues that knowledge loses its value and is often forgotten if a student cannot see its relevance.

In the interpretative view of teaching, the role of teachers is to assist students in making their own judgements through language and reflections. This requires ongoing dialog between teachers and students that builds on the specific contexts for language, which encourages each other's responses. What Barnes calls meaningful communication in a classroom occurs when teachers and students talk, argue, and model each other's language and gestures in the process of exchanging meanings. In these terms, meaningful communication requires an environment in which students are encouraged to offer a perspective different from and perhaps, counter, to a teacher's.In this way, students are able to clarify their own ideas. Barnes attempts to bridge the gap between teacher language and student language by advocating teachers shift from transmission to interpretation.

An interpretation approach to teaching considers writing part of a child's cognitive and personal development. It places the child at the center of the writing process. Writing is considered as a reflective process in which students shape and reshape their understanding of their world. Interpretive teachers support student writing development and knowledge by responding directly to the student in the form of questions and comments. Knowledge acquired through the interpretive approach to writing becomes something gained through socially created dialog between the teacher and the student.

Knowledge that is socially created produces what Barnes calls "action knowledge", which students incorporate into their own ideas about reality. It recognizes that learning occurs when students are asked questions by the teacher, or ask themselves questions, and then proceed with their own inquiry. Action knowledge is not the type of learning reported by teachers such as, "Johnny is doing well in English". Rather, it is the type of knowledge which escapes numerical assessment. Action knowledge considers what processes students use in knowledge acquisition and what students do with new understandings.

Action Knowledge and Exploratory Talk

According to Barnes, action knowledge comes from exploratory talk that students use in the acquisition of knowledge. Exploratory talk is not "rapping", but instead dialogic in nature and not judged by standards external to a student, such as examinations. Students' use of oral or written language in exploratory talk is never seen as esoteric. Exploratory talk does not have a prescribed conclusion in mind. The role of teachers in exploratory talk is to help students articulate their speech or writing. Exploratory talk, according to Barnes, allows a student to test out drafts of their oral and written language. Barnes notes that exploratory talk is negated by teachers, since students are often asked for final drafts.

Barnes' notion of English Language as communication contributes to Media Education, since it acknowledges a language learner as involved in learning how to communicate meaningful messages. It encourages students to talk about how they understand and interpret different types of discourse on their own. The teacher's role is to assist students in active exchanges with one another.

Moffett and Discourse

Moffett's definition of discourse builds on Britton's functions of language and Barnes' idea of communication. According to Moffett and Wagner (1976), communication builds on the disparity between sender and receiver in an exchange of information. They introduce the concept of discourse, which they define as:

> Discourse is any communication having a sender, receiver, and a message bound by a purpose. A discourse, for example, would be a conversation, a lecture, a letter, or journal, a poem or short story, ad or label (p. 12).

Penfield (1987) states that for successful language users, communication occurs in discourse events. She describes discourse events as:

> defined by custom or cultural convention, by the flow of topics or events within them, by social setting, by the social and personal relationships of the speakers involved in using them, and by many other variables as well (p. 13).

Moffett (1968) describes four different types of discourse: reflective discourse (i.e., conversation with oneself), interpersonal communication (i.e., between two people within speaking range), correspondence (i.e., discourse between acquaintances), and publication (i.e. impersonal communication to an unknown audience over an extended time and space). Each consecutive discourse is more selective and public than the previous one. The focus shifts from reflective and interpersonal to a larger, unknown subject. Communication abilities develop as a student moves through different discourses. Moffett suggests that experiences with different types of discourse enables students to discriminate between different forms of messages and their sources, to determine the value of a message based upon its origin, and to become familiar with composing for audiences they might or might not know. Students need opportunities to encounter, explore and practice how to use language to express experiences, through what he refers to as the universe of discourse. Children's use of discourse naturally moves from reflective to interpersonal. Moffett states that Language Arts curriculum should assist students in moving beyond those discourses to include correspondence and publication.

Language Arts and Media

English Language teaching as practised in schools was counter to Moffett and Wagner's (1976) conceptualisation of discourse. Moffett and Wagner, who defined literacy as being able to compose and comprehend in a variety of discourses, viewed English as a disjointed curriculum that confused literacy with ad hoc courses in the "art" of reading skills and word recognition (i.e., decoding), writing skills, listening skills and speaking skills (i.e., encoding). They criticised many of the practices in English teaching as limited to helping students acquire "high standards" in writing skills, instead of providing opportunities for students to use various types of discourse and forms of communication.

The focus on high standards led English teaching to favor what Moffett and Wagner described as the particle approach. The particle approach breaks language into sequential units, including words, sentences, and paragraphs. Students are then taught how to receive and reproduce these units in order to improve grammar, void of purpose and meaning. Moffett and Wagner believe that Language Arts teaching confuses grammar (i.e., errors in punctuation, sentence structure, etc.) with producing discourse in a relevant, realistic, imaginative, and meaningful fashion through effective expression. They recommended that effective expression is best taught through involvement with active discourse, such as conversing with others, role playing, choral reading, and participating in theatre. Moffett and Wagner refer to "raw experience" as a motivator for using language to express experiences for ourselves, and for those with whom we wish to communicate. This is similar to Britton's notion of expressive language. Raw experience recognizes student experience outside of school.

Discourse is any communication having a sender, receiver, and subject bound by a purpose, and can occur through oral, written, and visual language. Moffett provides a framework for analysing different forms of discourse: oral, written, and visual discourse includes song lyrics and slide tape narrations, poems or a story, a sculpture, and a film. Moffett's concept of discourse and its different types enables us to make the link between the Language Arts and media. For the first time in our discussion, language (i.e., discourse) includes more than just reading and writing print. Moffett argues students should learn discourse abilities through moving from interior dialog to socialised speech, to language recording and reporting, to generalising, to theorising, and through manipulation of various symbols systems, including speech, writing, gestures, music, and images.

For students to be literate in the different types of discourses, using various forms of media, they need to be given occasions to listen, speak, read and compose through oral, written, and visual discourse. The ability to compose in one form of communication enables a student to transfer language abilities to another. Through composing, students are able to understand the nature of language, and find out what various media are able to do, as well as how various media complement each other.

Acquisition and Learning:
Primary and Secondary Discourse

Gee (1996) amplifies Moffett's notion of discourse, using the terms primary and secondary discourse to distinguish what students already know from what they might be taught. Primary discourse is the basis for the acquisition and learning of other discourses later in life. As such, primary discourse is specific to the socio-economic experience of a child.

Secondary discourses "involve uses of language, either written, oral, or both, as well as ways of thinking, valuing and behaving and go beyond the uses of language of primary discourse, no matter what group we may belong to" (p. 152). Secondary discourses are acquired and learned through social institutions outside of a home (i.e., schools, the workplace and religious institutions). To this list we may add the mass media, the world of advertisements, and popular culture. Gee's notion of secondary discourses recognizes that discourse is embedded within specific socio-political institutions, which he calls "props" (p. 143). Props have the following implications for discourse:

1. Discourse is ideological in nature,
   involving dominant values and viewpoints.
2. Criticism comes from outside of dominant discourse.
3. Discourse is often opposing.
4. Discourse is empowering.

Gee's description of discourse is significant, since it extends Moffet's notion of discourse and reflects some of Willinsky's (1991) elements of postmodern literacy: postmodern literacy acknowledges oppositional texts found in popular culture forms and encourages the reading and writing of alternative texts; postmodern literacy is critical literacy that, through the use of language, promotes public consciousness of social, cultural and economic ideologies. Gee's distinction between acquiring and learning knowledge illustrates how vital it is for teachers to allow students to bring their understanding of their world in to a classroom and apply it to the learning process.

The notion that students make meaning through secondary discourse is reinforced by Halliday (1974). According to Halliday, the role of schooling is to help students develop an awareness of their social position. It is "by means of language that a person becomes potentially the occupant of a social role" (p. 10). He refers to this as the "functional approach of language" (p. 13).

Language that fosters meaning making adopts a socio-linguistic nature that, according to Halliday, involves "the encoding of a behavioral potential into a meaning potential" (1974, p. 19). The meaning potential Halliday refers to is not found within subject content, but rather emanates from the student. In essence, what is being referred to here is the notion that we each negotiate our own meaning of a message or a text.

Like Halliday, Anderson and Meyer (1988) argue that meaning making involves the interaction between communicants, content, and context. We are reminded here of Moffett and Wagner's notion of the role of purpose and context in discourse. However, traditionally teachers have considered language as a means to teach content rather than as an interactive process through which students construct meanings. Halliday, Anderson, and Meyer advocate that in order for discourse abilities to be developed, classrooms need to be interactive. This echoes Barnes' (1992) notion of interpretation teaching. Students must be given the opportunity to explore not only expressive and artistic forms of language, but also socio-cultural usages of language that students experience everyday, such as popular culture forms of language.

Knowledge of and Learning about Language

Doughty, Pearce, and Thornton (1976) extend Moffet's notions of discourse described earlier by including the context in which discourse takes place. According to Doughty, Pearce and Thornton, language is more than a standard form of writing or linguistic ability. Students come to school with a wide experience and familiarity with language that they use everyday. Doughty, Pearce, and Thornton refer to this as knowledge of language. However, they argue that learning about language involves more than familiarity. Learning about language includes using language to express and order one's experience, as well as understanding how to use language for different audiences in specific social occasions. The focus in the first part of learning about language is on the student who uses language for articulating his/her own experiences to him/herself. The second aspect of teaching about language is understanding how we use language in establishing our identity within social groups, as well as understanding how social contexts operate to create our social identity.

Doughty, Pearce, and Thornton outline three levels of social relationships. At one level, language is used in relationship to one's role and status as membership in a family or a community. Moving beyond the family and community, language is used as a means through which we maintain our identity outside or within larger social groups, such as in a crowd, or in an interview. The final and farthest away in terms of social context is the way we use language in relationship to social institutions, such as school and the workplace.

A student's ability to use language for the specific purposes and social contexts described above includes being aware of the active range of roles one must play and the social behaviors that others see as appropriate from someone in the different roles. The focus here is on the user of language who acts within and upon a social context.

However, as Doughty, Pearce, and Thornton point out, understanding the role of language in a social context also includes being conscious that our identities are also acted upon by the kind of language used during the course of interaction. They define literacy as, "the ability to draw on a wide experience of the language system in order to meet the particular occasions for using language" (p. 112). This definition is important for Media Education, since it argues that literacy includes the knowledge that students already have about language (wide experience) as well as the need for students to understand the specific purposes and contexts (particular occasions) in which language is used.

Some of the particular occasions described by Doughty, Pearce, and Thornton (1976) include using language to convey information, reporting events, making speeches, producing advertisements, and writing a radio or television script.

Doughty, Pearce, and Thornton agree with Britton's notion that language use in schools is mostly a transactional function of language. They observe, as Barnes did that teacher talk dominates schooling. Like Moffett, they criticize current English Language Arts teaching as largely skill building for formal learning situations in schools.

They refer to the kind of language used by teachers as the "language of the subject text book and public examination" (p. 17). Text book based language teaching is used as a model for good language. However, it leaves little opportunity for students to draw from their wide experiences of the language system. Reflection is sacrificed in search of the "correct" answer (Dias, 1992). Rather, a student's intelligence is gauged according to his/her ability to use standard text book language. In turn, students evaluate their own use and ability to use language on this model. The text book approach ignores one of the major premises of the Dartmouth Conference, which argued for language teaching that included the development of a child.

In place of a textbook approach to language teaching, Doughty, Pearce, and Thornton advocate that teachers help students to use language effectively in the process of articulating experience. Learning about language includes being able to name things, categorise abstract and general concepts, describe sensations, distinguish between fiction and reality, and express values and attitudes.

Doughty, Pearce, and Thornton also argue that learning about language involves understanding that language is used in different ways for different occasions, suggesting different audiences. Discourse occurs when there is an understanding that there is a real audience with whom one is engaged in a meaningful relationship. This is important, since it is the first time in our discussion reference is made to the consideration of a real audience who expect a specific kind of discourse. Doughty, Pearce, and Thornton argue that real audiences are an important part of what students have to know in learning about language.

Text, Author, Audience and Reader

Rosenblatt (1978) brings together much of the work discussed so far in this inquiry concerning the nature of language, the role of writers and readers, and how meaning is created in a message or a text. Her concept of a text goes beyond the symbolic structures and conventions. She states:

> Text designates a set or series of signs interpretable as linguistic symbols. The visual or auditory signs become verbal symbols, become words, by virtue of their being potentially recognisable as pointing to something beyond themselves (p. 12).

Reading includes responses to all kinds of texts, such as speech, statues or objects (i.e., media). A text includes a writer's intended message and a reader's aroused consciousness to that meaning. Rosenblatt argues that it is important to consider not only what a text brings to a reader, but what readers bring to a text. Her focus is on the reader instead of the producer of a text:

> Readers bringing to the text different personalities, different syntactical and semantic habits, different values and knowledge, different cultures, will under its guidance and control fashion different syntheses, live through different works (p. 122).

In the act of reading, the importance of a reader in creating meaning of a text has historically been neglected. From classical times, the focus in this act was on the text itself, and how well the text reflected or imitated reality. However, toward the end of the 1800s, society became more complex and uncertain of its own social reality and order. We may assume that the industrial revolution and the advent of mass media – such as newspapers and magazines – played a role in promulgating social uncertainty. This uncertainty resulted in the notion that a text did not stand alone. How well a text imitated or reflected reality was only as valid as the person who created it. Rosenblatt describes the role of a reader as an invisible eavesdropper (p. 2). The only way in which a reader could participate in a text was to express meaning in the author's terms. The reader merely decoded the message of the author. The reader was often judged by his/her ability to comprehend the text the author generated. Rosenblatt argues that throughout literary history, a reader has not been acknowledged as an active part in making meaning of a text.

In opposition to gauging a student's understanding of a text by how well he/she interprets what supposedly is a "correct" reading of a text (i.e., according to "authorial intent"), Rosenblatt stresses that a text does not act upon a reader. Instead, it is a reader who responds to a text. She refers to this as a "transactional process" (p. 18) in which a reader reconstructs meaning in a text according to the symbolic nature of the text, and the reader's past raw experiences. The reader selects elements from the text and then cuts and pastes to fit a context, a personality, and a level of meaning. How a reader makes meaning in a text is dependent on a reader's experiences with texts. According to Rosenblatt, "texts act as stimuli, blueprints and regulators" (p. 11). They are not fixed creations, but develop through collaboration and appropriation of texts which already exist. Dias (1992) echoes Rosenblatt's transactional notion. Dias argues that texts are not static unchanging entities, and that the traditional role of a teacher as one who establishes meaning in a text for students is counter to the transactional process. Similar to Willinsky's (1991) idea that texts in postmodern literacy develop through collaboration and appropriation of texts that already exist, a text is renewed in the transactional process that occurs between a reader and a text.

Aesthetic and Efferent Reading

Efferent Reading

All texts summon active readings, and thus active readers. The type of response activated is dependent on the nature of the text. Rosenblatt states that all reading is carried on in a form of experienced meaning through efferent and aesthetic reading. In efferent reading, the focus is on the information that a reader requires in order to carry out a specific function. The meaning is drawn outward from the reader. Efferent reading is characteristically practical. During efferent reading, a text acts upon a reader. Readers are not asked to call upon their life experiences and are not permitted to seek out a position (but are asked to call upon their references with similar texts). In this way, readers of an efferent text are not part of the sensual elements of a text. Reader and author share a common experience represented in a text, and consequently agree on the meaning conveyed. Dias (1992) comments that reading a text in order to answer predetermined comprehension questions is not the same as reading for one's own pleasure (p. 132). When a reader is asked to give a preferred reading of text rather than his/her own reading, not only is spontaneity lost, but also positioning oneself within a text becomes a forced rather than a personal, unconscious, and immediate reaction.

Aesthetic Reading

Rosenblatt's (1978) notion of "aesthetic reading" places the experienced meaning in full light of awareness, and involves the selective process of creating a work of art" (p. 75). The focus in aesthetic reading is what happens for a reader while the reading is going on. The text draws a reader inward to his/her own life experiences. Aesthetic reading entices a reader to become involved in the transactional processes described in the previous section. We cannot ignore our experience while reading a text any more than we can ignore our perceptions of the world around us. Aesthetic reading is selective, since a reader picks out information that has particular cognitive and emotional appeals.

Rosenblatt points out that the same text may be read either efferently or aesthetically, depending on whether a reader is acting in either of what Britton calls participant or spectator positions. As a participant, a reader is asked to perform or respond to a text in a specific way, efferently; for example, asking a student to name the characters or plot in a short story. As spectators, readers can consider how they felt about the believability of the characters or plot, thus reading aesthetically.

Rosenblatt stresses that students must be given opportunities to read aesthetically, so they will be able to engage in the transactional process of reading. In this way, they will realize their relationship with a text. She stresses that through aesthetic reading, students become producers of language by structuring and clarifying experience (p. 29). It is especially interesting to note that Rosenblatt believes that the purest of interpretations of a text are those made by what she calls an ordinary reader (p. 140). A text for an ordinary reader is a living entity to be experienced rather than analyzed. The ordinary reader does not secure cues from literary devices hidden within a text by the author. Ordinary readers make meaning in a text through emotions triggered by "socio-cultural settings" (p. 78). It is, thus, more important what a reader brings to a text rather than what a text brings to a reader.

Rosenblatt rejects what she calls the ideal reader of a text or a correct reading of a text (p. 140). Her notion of literacy is one that includes the transactional relationship in which a reader strives to become closer to the text, through the process of making more demands on texts and therefore on him/herself. By responding to a text in any form, oral, written, or visual, a reader is able to position him/herself within a literate world by making meaning. Rosenblatt thinks that education's responsibility lies in narrowing the gap between literacy designed for the ordinary reader and literacy designed for the elite (p. 142). In essence, she is arguing for the right of all readers to take responsibility for making meaning, and to participate on a level footing, without procedures which hinder literary transactions.

Rosenblatt's notion that readers actively create meaning of a text fits well with one of the basic premises of Media Education: audiences negotiate meaning of texts.

A New Model of Reading

McCormick, Waller, and Flower (1992), like Rosenblatt, argue that reading is not a passive activity but rather one in which a reader actively creates meaning (p. 6). They describe reading as:

1. An interactive process, produced by the interaction of the readers and texts.

2. Having both cognitive and cultural dimensions, that is, it is both an intellectual procedure that requires certain mental strategies and skills, and a cultural procedure, contingent upon your wider beliefs and assumptions.

3. The making of meaning is not merely a "subjective" or individual experience, because both readers and texts are deeply influenced by their socio-cultural context. Readers and texts alike are produced by (that is, they are the products of) their history and culture. Or, as some theorists like saying, they are "written" by their culture.

4. As a consequence of point 3, and because relationships between signifiers and signified are always culturally derived, certain readings might seem "correct" or even "intended by the author" in one socio-cultural context, but will not seem so across all cultural contexts. Thus, no text can be said to contain a single, fixed meaning, since readers' determinations of meaning are dependent on social, cultural, and literary assumptions that are in a continual state of change.

5. The readings readers develop from the text have implications for the other parts of our lives outside the classroom: there is no such thing as a purely "literary" reading (p. 9).

McCormick, Waller, and Flower's theory of reading conceives of texts as a system of signs. The term signs refers to objects, icons, or symbols that communicate, each comprised of a signifier and a signified. A reader's understanding of the physical existence of a word or image, the signifier, is not necessarily the same as the mental image, or the signified. Purves, Rogers, and Soter (1990) comment that semioticians have defined literacy as "thinking in sign systems, including not only oral and written sign systems, but also art, music, dance, and drama" (p. 86). Within these sign systems, we can include print, radio, film, television, man made environments, and popular culture artifacts.

Alvarado and Boyd Barrett (1992), editors of *Media Education: An Introduction*, contend that signs are useful tools for exploring the meaning of texts. Signs serve to explain how texts can have multiple meanings for readers, which McCormick, Waller, and Flower refer to as polyvalent readings. Polyvalent reading is similar to Rosenblatt's aesthetic reading, since it invites the transactional process in which readers give a variety of responses and interpretations to a text.

Polyvalent reading serves as the foundation for a "new model" of the reading process, which suggests that readers and texts each bring two categories of repertoires to bear on the reading transaction. Repertoires are comprised of combinations of ideas, experiences, habits, norms, and assumptions. One category of repertoire includes knowledge of language systems and literary conventions, such as medium, genre, mode, rhetoric, and codes. A second repertoire includes general ideological assumptions implicit in the moral ideas, beliefs, and values about the world at large. Reading is a transactional process involving a reader and a text, in which a reader brings to bear both a literary and general ideological repertoire to construct meaning from the text in which is embedded the producer's literary and ideological repertoire. Following from Rosenblatt's notion that readers negotiate meaning of texts, McCormick, Waller, and Flower's new model of reading is important for Media Education. It introduces the notions that texts are made up of signs that are socially and culturally constructed, have multiple meanings, and contain ideological and value messages.

A Shift in the Ideology of Literacy

In reviewing the developments in English Language Arts, especially since the Dartmouth Conference, one can see the evolution in thinking about the nature of English Studies. Because of the shift in emphasis from Composition and Literature studies (a Cultural Heritage and elitist model) to Language Arts (a New Literacy Model), there has been a concomitant shift in understanding of Literacy. This new understanding has best been characterised by Street (1984) in what he calls an "Ideological Model of Literacy". Its main features include the following assumptions:

* The meaning of literacy depends upon the social institutions in which it is embedded.

* Literacy can only be known to us in forms which already have political and ideological significance and it cannot, therefore, be helpfully separated from that significance and treated as though it were an "autonomous" thing.

* The particular practices of reading and writing that are taught in any context depend upon such aspects of social structure as stratification, and the role of educational institutions.

* The processes whereby reading and writing are learnt are what construct the meaning of it for particular practitioners.

* We would probably more appropriately refer to "literacies" than to any one single "literacy".

* Writers who tend towards this model and away from the autonomous model recognize between the analysis of any "autonomous" isolable qualities of literacy and the analysis of the ideological and political nature of literacy practice (p. 8).

CHAPTER FOUR
The Evolution of
Media Education Theory

This section has two objectives: to present a summary of the theoretical evolution of Media Education, and to discuss its concomitant curricular developments.

The Contribution of
Educational Technology to Media Education

Silverblatt (1995) states that the development of media technologies in the nineteenth and twentieth centuries provided for the dissemination of information and entertainment to mass audiences. The last sixty to eighty years has been designated by social historians as the period called the communication revolution (Finn, 1972). This time period has been marked by developments in printing, photography, motion pictures, radio, and television accompanied with research in psychology, mass communication, and education.

Inevitably, these media found their way into schools and influenced curriculum. The advent of the uses of audio visual technology began with films during the late 1920s and 1930s. Radio came into prominence during the late 1930s and 40s. As a result of the uses of these technologies to train large numbers of military and civilian personnel during World War II and the accompanying research on the effects of these technologies, there was a proliferation of audio visual technology, including still and motion picture projectors, slide sets, filmstrips, and a variety of sound and communication technology in schools after the war.

The result of bringing technology into schools established a climate in which media could be studied in its own right. It is my intention at this point to explore early attempts at Media Education. The first medium that was seriously examined as a medium itself within the context of formal education appears to be film. The reason for this was that film appeared to be most like literature. While films were being used in English studies during the 30s, for the most part English teachers in Britain and the United States viewed commercial cinema as a threat to serious literature. There were few attempts to deal with film as a literary experience, but rather as a means through which teachers could demonstrate superiority of classical literature over common forms of entertainment. The real motivation of English teachers during the early part of this century was to encourage students to reject lower class standards of popular media. They taught about media in order to discredit it, in the hopes that students would steer away from popular media texts.

Between 1929 and 1932, a series of studies were sponsored by the Payne Fund (Applebee, 1974). The focus of the studies was on the effects of motion pictures on children. The conclusion of the report emphasised that motion pictures played an important part in a young person's life, outside of school. The report prompted the NCTE to recommend that a list of classical films be developed based on classical texts, standards of appreciation outlined and a nation wide evaluation of the effectiveness of film study in schools be carried out. The outcome of theses recommendations demonstrated that not only film, but also newspapers and magazines could be adopted to English studies (Applebee, 1974).

In Britain during the 1920s and 30s, Media Education developed from a classical tradition of literary criticism. The approach taken was based on the premise of immunising students against popular texts such as films so that they would turn toward reading the classics, high quality print literature (Buckingham, 1990; Halloran and Jones, 1992; Masterman, 1985, 1994). The innoculatory notion of Media Education found its genesis in the 1938 *Report on Secondary Education (Spens Report)* which stated that "the cinema and . . . the public press . . . subtly corrupt the taste and habit of a rising generation" (cited in Halloran & Jones, 1992, p. 11) and in the writings of F.R. Lewis and Denys Thompson.

The Leavis and Thompson Influence

Democratisation, urbanisation, education, increased income, leisure time, and industrialisation resulted in the emergence of the middle class in the late eighteenth century (Silverblatt, 1995). With the growth of the middle class and the development of media technologies during the late nineteenth and twentieth centuries, came the development of a new form of popular entertainment (i.e., popular culture). Nye (1978) defines popular culture as:

> Those productions, both artistic and commercial, designed for mass consumption, which appeal to and express the tastes and understanding of the majority of the public, free of control by minority standards. They reflect the values, convictions, and patterns of thought and feeling generally dispersed through and approved by American society (p. 22).

Historically, popular culture has been considered by elite cultures as a threat to cultural authority. According to Halloran and Jones (1992), Leavis and Thompson's publication, Culture and Environment (1933), reflected a cultural mistrust of mass media by educators as well as many others in the middle and upper classes of society. Their thinking was that industry was the product of technological and mechanistic capitalism. Since the mass media are products of technology, they promulgated the decline of cultural values and the deterioration of language by preventing society from meeting human needs that are associated with work, nature and community. On the other hand, great cultural works were viewed as expressions of personal values. Leavis and Thompson considered that popular culture artifacts, which were mass produced and lacking any real challenges, distracted young people from the genuine forms of high culture such as classical literature. Their views are illustrated in the following quote:

> Those who in school are offered (perhaps) the beginnings of education in tastes are exposed, out of school, to the competing exploitation of the cheapest emotional responses; films, newspapers, publicity, in all its forms, commercially catered fiction all offer satisfaction at the lowest level, and inculcate the choosing of the most immediate pleasures, got with the least effort . . . We cannot, as we might in a healthy state of culture, leave the citizen to be formed unconsciously by his environment; if anything like a worthy idea of satisfactory living is to be saved he must be trained to discriminate and to resist (pp. 3-5).

Leavis and Thompson viewed English studies – through a response to "serious" literature and through written and spoken language – as society's best defense against the decline of old values, and the encroachment of capitalism. Young people were to be inoculated so that they would be provided with the skills necessary to discriminate between high culture and those products produced by the mass media. The position stemming from the innoculatory principle was also applied to cinema. Masterman (1980) notes that the importance of Leavis and Thompson was not their moralistic stance, but rather their role in bringing media texts into classrooms.

The innoculatory approach to teaching mass media continued in Britain and the United States into the late 1950s and 60s (Hoggart, 1959; Hall and Whannel, 1964). Concern about the impact of the mass media was expressed in *The Crowther Report* (1959). The report warned that:

> Because they [mass media], are so powerful they need to be treated with the discrimination that only education can give . . . There is also . . . a duty on those who are charged with the responsibility for education to see that teenagers, who are at the most insecure and suggestible stage of their lives, are not suddenly exposed to full force of the mass media , without some counterbalancing assistance (vol. 1, paragraph 66).

Buckingham (1990) cites two examples of current concerns about the effects of mass media. Moral panic refers to the view that media are contributing factors in the decline of moral values. Foremost, are concerns such as violence and pornography in television and movies. Marie Winn's book, *The Plug in Drug* (1985) focuses on the ways in which television affects children's thought processes and interaction with their families. Also, Elizabeth Thoman (1990), executive director of the Center For Media and Values, wrote in the quarterly newsletter *Connect* that:

> the mass media tend to favor instant gratification and the quick fix, confrontation over communication, image over substance and limitless material gain for the simple reason that, well, it's progress (p. 1).

Media Education: The 1960s

Ironically, the Leavis and Thompson practice of encouraging newspapers, advertisements, and journals being brought into schools for innoculation purposes played an important role in advancing the teaching about various forms of popular entertainment in schools during the 1960s and 70s. By the 1960s, teaching about media became part of the English curriculum (Buckingham, 1993b). Masterman (1985) notes that English teachers of the 1960s could not accept the innoculatory concept, simply because many of these teachers had grown up with the electronic media, and therefore considered Leavis' elitism and devotion to high culture as a confrontation with their own appreciation of popular culture. Also, the 1960s saw the introduction of communication courses at universities in both North America and Britain. Because they were students in university communication courses, teachers came to realize that films produced by specific directors, initially from France, then the rest of Europe, and finally from the United States, had as much value as classical literature. Consequently, teachers began to bring their training in communication studies into English and Fine Arts classrooms. Teaching against the media became teaching about the media. The move from innoculation to discrimination is referred to by Masterman (1985) as a shift to the Popular Culture Paradigm. An illustration of this shift is reflected in the *Newsom Report.*

The Newsom Report
and Dartmouth Conference

The hesitation of English teachers to teach media is expressed in several reports. In 1963. *Half Our Future (the Newsom Report)* was part of a broad re-evaluation of education at all levels in Britain. The *Newsom Report* focused on secondary schools, and was influenced by the child centered approaches of Dewey (Alvarado, 1977). The Report made "a strong claim for the study of film and television in their own right as powerful forces in our culture and as significant sources of languages and ideas" (paragraph 474). It stated:

The English lesson . . . is most likely to offer those opportunities which allow adolescents to write out of themselves what they are not always prepared to talk about . . . Teachers whose sole standard is correctness can dry up the flow of language and shackle creative and imaginative writing before it is under way (p. 157).

While it was favourable toward the use of mass media in schools, it still presented a Leavisite view of film and television as a teaching tool to be used to counter act the corrupting influences of the mass media. Claiming that education's approach toward the mass media should be discriminatory, the report suggested that newspapers and magazines be studied in secondary schools, and that film and television supplement literary texts (Halloran & Jones, 1992; Masterman, 1980; Murdock & Phelps, 1973). The Report stated:

We need to train children to look critically and discriminate between what is good and bad in what they see. They must learn to realize that many makers of films and of television programmes present false or distorted views of people, relationships, and experience in general, besides producing much trivial and worthless stuff made according to stock patterns (paragraph 475).

Some English teachers held the view that a limited number of films could be considered as art forms and used as criteria by which to judge "immoral" films. Generally speaking, a thematic approach was used that attempted to connect the major moral precepts of "good" films with the students' life experiences. The report proposed that films that demonstrated good moral values – and which therefore were to be considered as art forms – could be used to develop a student's judgment and discrimination:

By presenting examples of films selected for the integrity of their treatment of human values, and the craftsmanship with which they were made, alongside others of mixed or poor quality, we can not only build up a way of evaluating but also lead pupils to an understanding of film as a unique and potentially valuable art form in its own right, as capable of communicating depth experience as any other art form (paragraph 476).

The Newsom Report was significant in that it advocated a serious consideration of popular texts in schools and an application of literary criticism to film criticism. This development provided an opening for media to be integrated into English and Humanities courses. It is important to note that at the time the Newsom Report was written, television was becoming popular. However, the Report dismissed television, since it believed that it lacked virtues associated with high culture. In effect, the report judged each of the mass media as separate entities based on their aesthetic and virtuous qualities. Masterman (1980) remarks that the advice of the report resulted in a disjointed approach to Media Education, so that there was a separate course in television, film, radio, print, etc.

Three years later, and a continent away, the participants at the Dartmouth Conference (1966) suggested that all media were vital to classroom instruction, so that students would be able to express their experiences orally, written and visually. Muller (1967) comments that English teachers at the Dartmouth Conference realized that they could not "treat the mass media simply as the enemy" (p. 138), and that they would do better to work with the new art forms, good and bad. The Dartmouth participants, many of whom were from Great Britain, suggested that as teachers, their role was to help students to be more discriminating consumers of media. While the Dartmouth Conference influenced the use of mass media texts in schools, it did not provide direction as to how Media Education should be taught.

1970s

Despite the increased use of media as a result of the Popular Arts Paradigm, Media Education by the mid 1970s had changed little since the 1920s (Masterman, 1985). Masterman lists three reasons for this. First, English teachers, for the most part, still clung to innoculatory ideologies. Second, these ideas were based on a notion of high versus low culture (i.e., between classical texts versus popular media texts). Third, the criterion used to distinguish between high and low culture were based on a teacher's subjective opinion. Since many teachers in the 1960s came from middle class backgrounds whose values were based on conservative notions of family, religion and loyalty, their analysis of television and films reflected many of their own middle class values. Many students who came from lower class backgrounds were prevented from sharing their own interpretations. This alienated many students, just as Standard English alienated students in English classes. Finally, Media Education up to the mid 1970s failed because film, especially the "classic", was principally used as the object of study, even though the most influential and popular medium for students in the 1960s and 70s was television. In 1975, The *Bullock Report* (Department of Education and Science, 1975) recognized that students spent a considerable amount of time watching television. It supported the integration of television into the study of mass media. It advocated that television should be used as a disseminator of experience, and that a critical approach to it should be developed. While the *Bullock Report* may have been the spark that re-energised Media Education, a further reconceptualisation of media was necessary.

The Contribution of Structuralism and Semiotics to Media Education

The development of Media Education in the late 1970s can be attributed to the emerging interdisciplinary field of structuralism, which spawned the study of semiotics as an approach to understanding media (Alvarado & Ferguson, 1983; Masterman, 1985, 1994). Gibson (1984) quotes Scoles' definition of structuralism as "a system: a complete, self regulating entity that adapts to new conditions by transforming its features whilst retaining its systematic structure" (p. 12). Central to structuralist theory is the idea that structures or systems manage and define objects of study.

Structuralism's underlying principle, upon which all other structuralist principles build, is the notion of wholeness. The wholeness that makes up the structure of human behavior includes interactions with political institutions such as schooling and the media as well as our social position: class, gender, culture, and race. This can best be summed up by the phrase 'the whole is greater than the sum of its parts'. Ensuing from the notion of wholeness, structuralism's second principle is that reality lies in the relationship of the parts to the whole. For instance, meaning in texts is determined not by what individual words express, but rather by what words convey through their relationship to each other.

Structuralism has its original roots in the study of linguistics. In the late 1800s, sociolinguist Ferdinand Saussure rejected linguists' historical approach to the study of language. Saussure argued that language had to be examined in its present forms, through sign systems. That is, on the signifying practices of language. All forms of language are sign systems which express the conveyed meaning of the author and the interpreted meaning of the reader. Sign systems distinguish between what the sign denotes, the signifier, and the connotation of the sign, the signified.

Saussure's notion of sign systems established the field of semiology, which is "not restricted to linguistics, but would study all forms of communication in society..." (Gibson, 1984, p. 19).

While Saussure focused on written language, Barthes' *Elements of Semiology* (1967), *Mythologies* (1957), and *Image, Music and Texts* (1977) demonstrate how such non print texts such as toys, wrestling matches, football games, cinema, and a strip tease act can also be understood as sign systems. Gibson (1984) quotes Barthes:

> systems whose functions is not to communicate an objective, external meaning which exist prior to the system, but only to create a functioning equilibrium, a movement of signification . . . they signify 'nothing'; their essence is in the process of signification, not in what they signify (p. 100).

Barthes draws attention to the idea that media texts can be actively read through meaning conveyed in words, sounds, and images.

Gibson argues that "literature will be replaced by semiotics, for writing any writing, Shakespeare or advertising jingles, is merely different parts of a system which can be studied to discover how they work" (p. 100). Gibson makes the link between literature and Media Education. Literature, in structuralist terms, is considered as a system with its own conventions and customs. The role of structuralism in literature, and indeed in Media Education, is to:

underpin a whole range of structuralist activities: classifying within and between literary genres; identifying the fundamental dramatic situations; revealing the structures of fairy tales and myths; mapping the laws and functions of folk tales, demonstrating the various ways in which signs or language create an illusion of reality and hence convey meaning (p. 95).

Structuralism also presents the notion that all systems are subject to transformation. While maintaining universal laws of language, literature transforms itself as authors rewrite their own texts, and as readers reconstruct them. This fits with Media Education, which argues that meaning is created through a transactive process combining the intent of the author and the reader's interpretation.

Literary analysis seeks to make relationships between the elements of literature such as text, genre, convention, and device (Gibson, 1984). Likewise, Media Education builds on the concept that representations in media texts are not reflections of reality, but are an attempt to recreate reality. Structuralism maintains that the system must be studied synchronically in a snap shot approach. In the snap shot approach, we understand the system, literature or the media, by examining how the parts are related in a specific text, rather than considering language in an historical context. We can better understand media by exploring how meaning is created in a particular text.

Semiotic's notion of texts as sign systems underlies the fundamental principle of Media Education. The principle of non transparency asserts that "media are symbolic (or sign) systems which need to be actively read, and not unproblematic self explanatory reflections of external reality" (Masterman, 1985, p. 20). In order to be media literate, a student must be able to understand the sign and symbol system of media (Silverblatt, 1995).

Ideology

The signifying practices of structuralism and semiotics are responsible for Media Education's move away from innoculatory and discriminative practices toward understanding how values, beliefs systems, and attitudes are created in texts as dominant representations of reality (Silverblatt,

1995; Masterman, 1985, 1994). According to Hall (1996), media do not merely reflect society but rather promote the dominant ideology of a culture as a means of maintaining control.

Media Education attempts to expose the naturalness of media texts as ideological products of media control and power. Masterman's (1994) description of ideology as two dominant and yet opposing ideas, the explicitly political and the common sensed, unconscious, and unrecognized, links the power of media institutions with audience's acceptance of dominant ideologies. Considine and Haley (1992) state that most:

> audiences still perceive the media image as transparent, a sign that simply says what it means what it says. They therefore tend to dismiss any intensive explication as a case of reading too much into it (p. 3).

Buckingham (1990) expands the concept of ideology to include male dominant gender roles and racist attitudes. Students must have the opportunity to deconstruct the visual, audio and editing techniques, the rhetorical devices for example, in order to discover how meaning is constructed and transmitted in cultural texts such as film, television and shopping malls. It is based on the notion that all languages, oral, written, and visual, operate as sign systems which, ".. can be read in many ways; each text contains within itself the possibility of an infinite set of structures" (Culler 1975, quoted in Gibson, 1984, p. 100). Buckingham, Fraser and Mayman (1990) suggest the following analytical procedures which enables students to recognize ideological messages:

1. Express initial response to a given text.
2. Identify and describe the different elements composing this text.
3. Identify the most prevalent associations and meanings for each of these elements.
4. Combine these associations/meanings together to suggest the dominant ideological meaning of the text.
5. Compare this meaning with other instances of the same category of text in order to arrive at conclusions about their overall ideological function.

In the process of deconstructing rhetoric to reveal ideology, a student discovers how a text is organized, and explores how its meaning combines with their personal experiences (Williamson, 1981). Readers/viewers move beyond the dominant ideologies of the original text to consider issues of ideologies of resistance, production, and consumption within a socio-political and historical context.

1980s

Alvarado and Ferguson (1983) state:

> Those who favoured the introduction of media studies into the curriculum argued that it was ridiculous that the major social, political and cultural form of communication in the twentieth century civilisation should be ignored by a curriculum inherited from a nineteenth century education (p. 24).

It is only within the last decade that Media Education has developed from fragmented courses in television, film, advertising, radio, etc. to a disciplined program of integrated principles, concepts, methodologies, and pedagogy. The writings of Masterman and Buckingham of England, Quin and McMahon in Australia, Dick of Scotland, and Duncan of Canada influenced the development of Media Education curricula based on the new attitude toward the media. These curricula were, in part, the result of grassroots pressure from teachers in Scotland and England who began to realize that the new media were a source of motivation for students. These teachers influenced the writing of the *DES Report: Popular Television and Schoolchildren* (Department of Education and Science, 1983) in England, which stressed that specialist courses in Media Studies in schools are not enough, and that all teachers should include television studies in their classrooms. The recognition that the media could be a valid field of study in schools and the development of new curricula in Media Education led to the need for a systematic way of teaching media.

Critical Framework and Key Concepts

Eddie Dick (1990) provided a model (*Figure 2*) for the initial framework of Media Education.

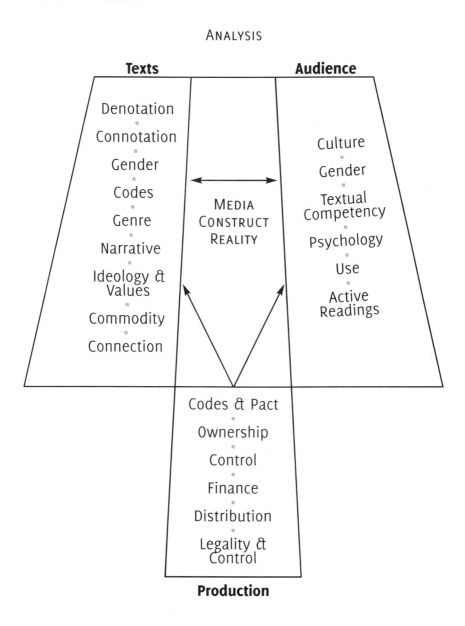

Figure 2

There have been several variations of the model in *Figure 2*, such as those developed in Ontario and Aspen. However, most of these have remained true to Dick's original conception (Shepherd, 1993). The frameworks are significant, since they provide teachers with the means for both educators and their students to coherently explore media. All the frameworks share common elements: text, audience, industry (referred to in some models as production), and an underlying premise that all media texts are constructions (Masterman, 1985, 1994).

This premise states that media do more than reflect reality. It contends that books, television programs, films, newspapers, radio programs, advertisements, and other cultural artifacts are actively produced. Media Education enables students to become aware of the social, cultural, political, and economic implications of media messages in order to interpret the ways in which media actively construct reality. It requires that students deconstruct media products in order to identify and examine not only the variety of techniques and rhetorical strategies used to create them, but also the cultural practices, ideas, and values vested in them. It aims to have students develop an awareness of the multiplicity of motivations, controls, and constraints that those who construct media products are subject to, and the sources – economic, political, technical and social – of these influences. It seeks to develop an understanding that the meanings of these constructed messages resides as much in the individuals who read media texts as they do in the texts themselves, that the process of interpretation of media messages is highly selective and contingent on cultural, environmental, and psychological factors (Emery et al., 1995).

Production:
Sources, Origins, and Determinants of Media

Cowles and Dick (1984) suggested that Media Education should begin in a classroom with exploring the commercial aspects of media. As cultural artifacts, media representations are produced, owned, and controlled by individuals and organizations.

The process of constructing media texts is influenced by the powers and motives of ownership; that is, media texts have embedded in them the dominant ideology of capitalism and private property. Furthermore, media producers are also subject to constraints: technological, legal, and economic codes and practices that may mitigate the messages of the texts themselves. The objective of exploring production is to help students understand the relationship among these dimensions of media production, including an understanding of the infrastructures of media monopolies, their creation, ownership, control and relationship to other independent media, how media ownership influences content, and how the media industry is regulated (Masterman, 1985, 1994; Silverblatt, 1995).

Texts: Media Rhetoric

Texts, according to Masterman (1985), include books, posters, clothing, advertisements, and public environments as well as television programs and films. Texts are constructed by producers using specific rhetorical devices and practices, and are reconstructed by audiences as they read them. The producer of the text presents what is inevitably selected, and presents partial representations as true, rational, authentic, and necessary. Media rhetoric is the ensemble of decisions and determinants that media producers select in order to construct meaning in a text. For example, a director may decide that a specific shot, selection, and editing of a sequence, the gender, age, race of a character or music tempo may produce a desired meaning in a television or film text. The interaction of signs, such as the camera shot, the denotation of the person or object, and the mood or environment create signifying units. Since the interpretation of a text is a social and cultural construct based on the manner in which the signs denote or connote meaning, a reader must be familiar with the uses of the codes and conventions specific to each medium and genre produced by the systematic shaping of rhetorical practices (Buckingham ,1994; Masterman, 1985, 1994; Lusted, 1991).

Ideology is embedded in any text. The concept of ideology is elusive, and therefore problematic in Media Education. Masterman (1994) states, it can refer:

in one definition, to any explicitly political (and generally doctrinaire and inflexible) set of beliefs (e.g., as in fascist or Marxist ideologies), in another, to its opposite, the realm of common sense, as manifested in our taken for granted beliefs and everyday language (p. 37).

Ideological analysis at the school level is difficult, since the only culture students know is the one that they inhabit (Quin, 1994). Thus, they are unaware of alternative or contradictory ideologies. Media Education encourages students to question the taken for granted, dominant ideologies of media texts through disclosing the rhetorical devices and practices used in the process of constructing the ideological meaning. Students can then move from what a text denotes, its descriptive state, to a rendering that connotes meaning that is socially and culturally constructed. As Quin and McMahon (1992) note, the role of a teacher is to help students discriminate between texts and contexts, as well a between image and cultural context.

Audience

Media Education emphasises the role of audiences actively creating meaning from a text, rather than merely receiving it (Lusted, 1991; Worsnop, 1994). Silverblatt (1995) reminds us that the reception theory recognizes that an audience may reach a different reading than the "preferred" (i.e., the author's intended message). Students and teachers can explore the ways in which responses to texts differ, and what contributes to the differences: culture, gender, race, class, experiences with similar texts, psychological profile, predisposition, interest level, stage of development. Knowing how they and others respond to texts assists students in finding how audiences accept, resist, or negotiate the meanings embedded in texts. Masterman (1985, 1994) points out that in the past, media teachers expected consensual and relatively consistent responses from their students; however, they are now likely to expect diversity. Students should be encouraged to negotiate their own meanings, possibly disputing not only media's values, but the teacher's as well.

The Contribution of Cultural Studies

The key concepts described in *Figure 2* (p. 79) reflect the developments that took place in English Language Arts, structuralism, and semiotics, as described earlier. One other contribution to Media Education has been that of cultural studies.

While Richard Hoggart (1959), David Morley (1980), John Fiske (1989), and Stuart Hall's (1996), and work in cultural studies in the last four decades have influenced Media Education, with the exception of Giroux (1983), relatively few people within cultural studies have realized its application to Media Education. However, media educators in Britain, Australia, and Canada have recognized the contribution of cultural studies to Media Education. Buckingham (1990) argues that cultural studies offers Media Education a theoretical approach to cultural production, in particular access to youth culture.

Masterman (1985) suggests that the cultural studies model of Media Education is essential for economic and political awareness. Quin and McMahon (1992) comment that Media Education must include the study of the media's socio-political context, as well as the links between the political structures, media policy, and cultural products. Mitchell (in Emery et al., 1995) states that cultural studies:

> takes as its central questions those which pertain to the texts on the other side of the line of Shakespeare, as well as questions about how the line ever got there in the first place: who draws it, why? How is it maintained? Cultural Studies is not about taking 'low culture' texts and trying to elevate them to canonised status, nor is it necessary about justifying the reading of low culture texts by investigating the ways in which they somehow serve as some sort of subversive reading. An important component of what Cultural Studies is all about is to explore the definition of what constitutes the texts of Cultural Studies. The focus is on a broader definition of what constitutes a text. (p. 7).

By not restricting itself to canonised texts such as classical literature, the cultural studies model of Media Education enables media educators and their students to question what defines culture, and more specifically, to build on children's knowledge of popular culture texts, such as television programs, romance novels, magazines, toys and shopping malls. Cultural studies positions Media Education so that the focus is on the relationship between the students and his/her identity within a culture.

Media Education Issues and Approaches

Issues

Despite a fair degree of agreement among Media Education curricula regarding content, there is some debate regarding the place of Media Education in the curriculum, how the curricula are to be implemented, and the general approaches to teaching that ought to be employed. The areas of dispute appear to be:

1) Whether Media Education should be a separate subject of the curriculum, whether it should be part of English studies, or whether it should it inform the study of all subjects of the curriculum
(Buckingham, 1990; Masterman, 1985, 1994).

2) What is the value of student production to a Media Education program relative to analysis?

On one hand, it is argued that student production has relatively little value to Media Education, because students focus on technological expertise rather than the concepts of the critical framework (Masterman, 1985). On the other hand, recent work by Ferguson (1981), Grahame (1990), Stafford (1990), (Emery et al., 1995), Ellis (1993), and Buckingham and Sefton-Green (1994) suggests that student production of media texts should be a central and indispensable part of the teaching about media. Production work invites students to become reflective about their own learning, as well as provides students the opportunity to discuss what they already know about popular culture texts.

Generally speaking, the following approaches are typical of those featured in the Ontario Media Literacy curricula.

Approaches

The inquiry method provides students with skills required to formulate questions, research information, collect data, and analyse the results of their inquiries in order to articulate the meanings of their investigations to themselves and others.

Building on the work of Robert Ennis (1962), the critical thinking approach enables students to reflect on the producer's point of view in a media text and to compare it with their own. According to Duncan (1988), the "challenge is in fostering not only the skills but also the necessary habit of mind, the critical spirit, if you like, in both teachers and students" (p. 4). This approach, according to the Ontario Resource guide, includes: distinguishing between facts and value claims, determining reliability, determining accuracy, distinguishing between warranted and unwarranted claims, detecting bias, identifying stated and unstated assumptions, recognising logical inconsistencies, and determining strength of an argument (p. 15).

Piette (1995) has developed a set of criteria from the literature on critical thinking and has applied these to the analysis of several of the major Media Education curricula produced in Britain, Canada, Switzerland, and the United States. His conclusion is that more critical thinking approaches and teaching strategies need to be deliberately incorporated into Media Education programs.

Emery (1993) states that teachers need to provide the following opportunities for students learning about media: they need to problematize what students know about media by helping them articulate and question their underlying assumptions. Teachers need to assist students in finding information, as well as provide resources and skills that will allow students to resolve their own inquiries. Teachers need to promote student understandings and skills that will help in their production and analysis of texts (p. 4).

Media Education Pedagogy

Media Education pedagogy is critical pedagogy (Giroux and McLaren, 1989) that offers students the opportunity to question meaning and create meaning based on their own interaction with media texts found outside of formal schooling (i.e., popular culture). Students are invited to actively explore socially and culturally constructed representations. Buckingham (1993) views Media Education as demystification which, through analytical processes, students question and challenge the non transparency and non neutrality of texts, including cultural and economic policies of institutions such as media and schooling.

These demystifying practices develop consciousness awakening about how media codifies experience and shapes meaning. Becoming conscious of how reality is constructed (in texts) enables students to analyse and create print and non print texts within specific contexts.

Freire (1990) refers to conscious awakening as conscientization. Conscientization enables a student to reflect objectively on his/her own reality and position. Students question not only those areas in a text that are obvious, but also those ideological issues which are not so transparent. By recognising and participating in both sides of a text (i.e., authors and readers), students question not only the text but also question – and reevaluate, if necessary – their own and other previously accepted understandings of reality. Through problem posing, ideological exploration, Media Education pedagogy provides opportunities for students to become conscious of media texts as powerful producers of dominant ideology. Buckingham (1993a) cites the example of objective analysis of racist or sexist stereotypes which "liberate us from the false ideologies these representations are seen to support and promote" (p. 285). This type of analysis is characteristic of what Freire (1970, 1990) describes as liberatory education in which "the teacher of the students and the students of the teacher cease to exist and a new term emerges: teacher student with student teachers" (p. 67). Media Education pedagogy that develops conscientization, and liberatory education redefines pedagogical relationships.

Media Education has its foundation in progressive pedagogy. At the center of Media Education Curriculum is the child (Shepherd, 1993).

Unlike traditional teaching, Media Education is student-centered; it promotes autonomy through active collaborative group work, using enquiry, discussion, and practical project production (Masterman, 1985, 1994). Students and teachers work individually and collectively as co-learners, through a process of debate, negotiation and consent. Media Education pedagogy acknowledges that students possess a wide knowledge of the media gained outside the classroom, and it argues against the idea that students are repositories that teachers deposit information into, a process referred to by Freire (1970, 1990) as the banking concept of education which "maintains and even stimulates the contradiction between teacher and student" (p. 46).

Inviting students to bring their own popular cultural texts alters a classroom, since it requires specific modes of teaching and learning between teacher and student, student and teacher, and student and student. According to Masterman (1985):

> Teaching effectively about the media demands non hierarchical teaching modes and a methodology which promotes reflection and critical thinking whilst being as lively, democratic, group focused and action oriented as the teacher can make it (p. 27).

Masterman's non-hierarchical pedagogy advocates assisting students to articulate what they know, as well as to realize the underlying questions that arise from student knowledge. Media teachers relinquish the position as providers of absolute truths and answers as well as being keepers of knowledge, and become co-researchers. In non-hierarchical pedagogy, the teacher's role is to navigate student learning without constraining, to prompt without making solutions obvious, and to enable students to learn without giving into the urge of making the learning neat and predictable. As navigator, a Media Education teacher selects the object of study of which s/he knows, but relearns as a co learner with students (Shor & Freire, 1987).

Media Education has a distinctive epistemology, in which knowledge is not so much deposited upon students as they actively create it through a process of investigation and dialog (Masterman, 1994, p. 59).

Despite the fact that there are essential conceptual differences between English Education and Media Education (Buckingham, 1990), historical, cultural, social and theoretical connections exist amongst English Language Arts teaching and Media Education, based on the relationship between language and postmodern literacy to texts, readers, writers and audiences. The preceding demonstrates a shift from an early, dominant class-based notion of literacy that included the ability to read and write certain literary fiction texts to a more democratic and broader perspective of literacy, which included a whole range of texts and different discourses and contexts in which individuals participate. That is,

> the notion of knowledge about language has a considerable potential for progressive English teachers, and connects to Media Education in some very productive ways (Buckingham, 1990, p. 22).

Media Education, like English Language Arts, is concerned with fundamental questions of language as a form of communication, in which meaning is conveyed or signified in three kinds of discourse: oral, written and visual. Each discursive form of language has its code or grammar and ways of codifying reality which must be learned in order for a student to "read" the text. Thus, literacy and a development of literacy about the media require an awareness of rhetoric including conventions, codes, genre, and narrative. The ability to transfer language into different forms of discourse and into different situations is an essential element of literate behavior. Bazalgette (1991) writes:

> Most people agree that fully literate readers bring many understandings to a text: that they can recognize what kind of a text it is, predict how it will work, relate it to other texts in appropriate ways. They can thus understand it critically, enjoying its pleasures, engaging with its arguments, reading between and beyond the lines (p. 90).

Every medium can be thought of as a language. Every medium has its own way of organising meaning, and we all learn to "read" it, bringing our own understandings to it, and extending our own experience through it.

Language Arts and Media educators and theorists – such as Dixon, Britton, Barnes, Moffett, Rosenblatt, Flower, Masterman, Buckingham, and others – help to redefine literacy based upon the distinctive and complementary roles that oral, written, and visual discourse play in understanding the social/personal growth of a student, the teaching/ learning environment, how meanings are constructed in different media, and audiences' different interpretations of the same text. These discourses occur within social, cultural, political, and ideological contexts. Furthermore, these socio-cultural contexts shape audiences and how they interact and reconstruct discourse. An important aspect of literate behavior is the ability to be aware of the nature of ideologies and the ways in which they are communicated.

Non-print visual media can be thought of in the same way that we think of print. The concept that enables us to think this way is that print, visual images, and sounds are signs.

Linguists (e.g., Saussure), semiologists (e.g., Barthes) as well as Language Arts educators (e.g., McCormick, Waller, and Flower) have much in common. Semiology acknowledged the media (i.e., print and non-print texts) as systems or structures which reflect a deeper sense of the interrelationships between a literary and visual text, how language works, and how meanings are communicated in different forms, for different purposes, and for different audiences. Further, although Dias' research dealt exclusively with poetry, it has applications to all kinds of texts and demonstrates an approach to reading and textual analysis in which meaning resides within the reader/viewer.

The above establishes not only the theoretical associations of English Language Arts and Media Education, but also identifies the social dynamics of the classroom in which students and teachers participate in the learning process as co-learners. Britton's notion that students function in the expressive mode implies a pedagogy in which students have more opportunity to express their understandings through themselves. This is very closely allied to Barnes' notion of the interpretation teacher. Both these concepts are comparable with Masterman's non-hierarchical teaching. This is illustrated in the following discussion with the ACE students:

J.R.: Media changed for me in understanding since I've been in this program. Before I started, I just watched it. Now I question some of it. Like why they did it, or how they did it in this way. And now, after the media course, I can understand. Like in movies, it can be an action or romance, whatever. Like how different shots can change the mood of things. Like a close up or a far away shot can make it seem like a change of time. Well maybe not a change of time, but different feelings. I practised angle shots; you can understand how it works, how they do it. I don't watch tv anymore, it kind of destroyed it, when I watch it. It ruins everything for everyone else.

Me: You mean when you watch with some one?

J.R.: Yeah. Like I know how to do that, or I'd like to know how to do that. And when I know how it's done, I try to explain it to them. I find different foul ups that they made.

Me: Anything else?

J.R.: Like covert commercials, commercials that are hidden in a movie or a show. Like 7-UP. They were showing this place, I don't remember where it was, but anyhow, you could see the big 7-UP. They tried to hide it, but you could see the red circle.

Me: What about working on the projects?

J.R.: Um . . . I know that I'm the kind of person who can't sit in a class room and take notes. The projects . . . I can't just research from the book to paper, writing it down, putting it in my own words, typing it up and handing it in. It's not me. What I like doing is going out, researching it, interviewing people, finding out exactly what I want to find out. Sometimes it doesn't work out that way, but that's what I like to do. I'm also not fond of working independently. I'd rather work as a team. If I do 50%, the other person catches up with the other 50%.

Me: Do you think working on projects in class has helped your learning?

J.R.: Well, you understand what . . . when you come back with your project you can say, hey look, this is what I learnt. I'm not just saying it, I'm proving it to you. 'Cause a lot of people don't like not having physical proof. These are the people I interviewed, this is what I found out. It even shows how the project is made from explaining the project, all the way to when it's finished. And it's done not to the teacher's satisfaction, but to our satisfaction. It's a good feeling handing in something like that. I did this. I'm proud of this. It also shows that someone has the initiative to get off their butt and make a movie (student produced video). And why can't I do it!

The Role of Teacher/Researcher

What I know about teaching at-risk students using Media Education and media technology is through induction, that is, by how I perceive and make sense of what occurs in my classroom on a daily basis. The approach that I take reflects what Mayher (1991) refers to as "uncommon sense learning", the outcome of intentional or purposeful action, that is neither linear, neat, nor packaged. It also reflects the pedagogical intuitions and theories that have served me well in my teaching, especially in the ACE Program.

Unquestionably, there are times when it seemed like I had dual personalities. At times I am more than a teacher, living the mundane, everyday teaching routines. At other times, I unyieldingly following accepted methodological designs. Patton (1990) succinctly reflects my thinking here. He argues that the best a teacher researcher can do is his/her very best, fairly representing the data, and communicating what the data reveals given the purpose of the inquiry. By this, Patton does not imply that there are no rules, merely that procedures are not rules. The qualitative inquiry depends on skills, training, insights, and capabilities of the research.

I taught the ACE students everyday, all day. My students and I did more than co-exist. As I stated earlier, I believe this was an advantage for my teaching overall. Together, we were a community within the larger school population. For some students, I was just one more teacher that they had to endure on the way out of school. For others, I was a teacher, surrogate parent, social worker, and a confidant. An exhausting number of roles, but this were inescapable considering the amount of time that we spent together, the entire school day, every day, for two years. Without question, we had a more intimate, intense relationship, beyond what is usual in a traditional school setting. Still, as illustrated in my comments below, I was troubled:

> So what's bothering me? I mean, I'm excited about the way the ACE Program is shaping up: the schedule, using media, and the kids' reaction to it, but it also irritated me. Maybe it's the fact that if I see this, why can't other teachers? Are we too set on teaching to the class? But that wouldn't account for it. Obviously, the reason is more embedded in teaching in mainstream than in alternative programs. But just think. If we got away from focusing on literacy in a narrow, print-oriented sense, then maybe students like mine could join with regular students in mainstream classes.

CHAPTER FIVE
The Literate Behavior
of the ACE Students

In this chapter, I discuss both the Literate Behavior of Reading and the The Literate Behavior of Writing of the ACE Students using examples from my classroom practice.

The Literate Behavior of Reading consists of three experiences, each of which is a chronological account of the reading by ACE students of two short films and a feature length video. The experiences took place in, more or less, the sequence presented. In real time, each took place in approximately one morning: three hours. Our class schedule enabled us to work for sustained periods on any one project, and involved the same group of students.

The Literate Behavior of Writing consists of two media projects the ACE students undertook, and are organised around the activities of the project, rather than presented chronologically. The projects spanned several weeks, and involved two different groups of students.

The Literate Behavior of Reading

The Apprentice

I was asked by a colleague – who was working in the marketing department of the *National Film Board of Canada* at the time – to develop a lesson plan for a short-nine-minute animated video entitled *The Apprentice*. I previewed the video several times. Indeed, it took several viewings before I was able to "read" it comfortably, although – as you shall see – not as well as I thought. Embarrassed, I told my colleague of my difficulty reading the film. She admitted that she also had some difficulty following the text.

The bizarre nature of *The Apprentice*, and the fact that it seemed to be aimed at an audience younger than the ACE students, made me apprehensive about using it. Still, since there was no dialog, it presented a good opportunity for my students to demonstrate what they had learned about "reading" visual texts. Earlier in the year, we had studied television and film language, such as the use of different camera shots, angles, and movement. The only other connection I could make to my students was that the story involved an apprentice and a teacher. Since the ACE students participate in On-the-Job Training twice a year, they are, in many ways, modern day apprentices.

The Narrative

The Apprentice is an animated film on video, set in mediæval times. The narrative focuses on the adventures of a teacher and his apprentice as they travel across the countryside. In the course of their travels, they come to a fork in the road. Ignoring the advice of the teacher, the apprentice decides to go on alone. Along the way, he is confronted by several obstacles. The story is divided into individual scenes, implied through fades to black, shifts in location, and jump shots. The fades to black operate in much the same way that turning pages in a book advances the story. Visual cues – including camera shots, angles, and movements – also carry the narrative.

Introducing the Text to the ACE Students

I introduced this visual text to the ACE students in the following manner. I explained that a friend of mine, who worked for an important government, national institution, the *National Film Board of Canada*, had asked me to provide her with some general feedback about a video she had just received. Several of the students questioned why she had chosen our class. I responded that aside from the fact that I was a friend of hers, she also knew that we had been exploring media production and analysis work.

Since I was not confident that I really had a "lesson plan", I decided not to be any more specific as to the kinds of feedback my colleague was looking for, hoping that something might develop on the spot. The most I would venture to ask the students was to tell me what occurred in the beginning, middle, and end of *The Apprentice*; in other words, to convey the narrative. I must admit, that I did not feel comfortable about being vague as to what I expected of them. This was due in part to the fact that I found it difficult to interpret the video myself. On the other hand, this was a pedagogically challenging opportunity to engage in what Masterman (1985) called teaching in a non-hierarchical fashion. Both the students and myself were going to co-investigate the video.

Initial, Silent Reading

The students' reading of *The Apprentice* developed in the following way:

As I have done with other print and non print texts, I initially began the activity very conventionally, by asking the students what the title of the video might suggest to them, engaging them in a discussion concerning the meaning of an apprentice, including similarities and differences among apprentices in "the old days" and their own on-the-job experiences, and what they thought the story might be about. The students easily related the concept of an apprentice to themselves.

I told the students that we would read/view the video without stopping, and without interruptions. Following this, we would discuss the plot and characters. Without any further introduction, the video was presented in its entirety. The students were then asked to express their initial responses to the film. As I had expected, many thought that the video had no point at all. Surprisingly, this actually added to their interest and curiosity. The classroom echoed to a chorus of, "Let's see it again." Surprised by their response, I rewound the tape and we viewed it again.

A Second Reading

My aim in the second reading was to slowly move them into broadening their comprehension of the video. This time, I asked them to tell me what happened at the beginning, middle and end. Many were only partially able to do so. Others related the plot in greater detail. What occurred next can best be described as serendipitous, or 'a teachable moment', as reflected in the following discussion:

Me: Can anyone tell me what the story is about?

M.B.: You don't get it Sir, do you?

Me: (somewhat embarrassed) No Mike, I guess I don't.

M.B.: (frustrated) O.K. Sir, rewind it again.

(After viewing the video again) Now do you get it?

Me: I'm not sure. Tell me.

T.S.: Sir, it's about a teacher and his student.

Me: Oh, I think I'm starting to see it now.

M.B.: It's like us. We're apprentices on our work study.

Me: So how do you know who the teacher and the student is?

M.B.: Rewind it again and stop it when I tell you.

I was really intrigued by M.B.'s comment: "It's like us. We're apprentices on our work study." His comment displays that he was responding affectively, through his personal relationship to the text, based on his prior work study experiences. Many of the other students had similar interpretations to M.B.'s.

I decided to admit to the students the difficulty I had reading the text. They were bewildered by my inability to see what seemed so obvious. Some were suspicious that I was acting naive so as to elicit their responses. I tried to tell them that in my private previewing, I had not read the video to the extent that they were now exhibiting.

I became excited that what I thought was going to be a fairly mundane and brief lesson, suddenly seemed to take on the possibility of being much more. I was not expecting the students to do make such personal connections. Remember, my initial idea was merely to have them tell me the beginning, middle, and end of the narrative.

Multiple Readings

I began to realize that the students were moving beyond initial first impressions of the story. Subsequently, I shifted the activity toward interpretation, getting the students to share what they felt the author of the video intended, and what meaning they found in the text.

With each reading and rereading of *The Apprentice*, the students analyzed and reconsidered their earlier readings. They developed associations and connections, which provided them with insights to their initial understandings, predictions and inferences.

Since I wanted to see what elements helped them read the video, I asked them to tell me what visual cues assisted them. In the next excerpt, several of the students were able to help me better understand the significance of some of the story elements:

Me: Hey, I'm really impressed. But what visuals or images helped you come up with these themes? What do you think the person, author of this video was trying to say? Did they seem to zoom into the 'good luck charm' around the teacher's neck?

J.R.: You still don't get it, do you Sir? Look, rewind it back to the tree. (tape is rewound). O.K. (sarcastically) Now fast forward it to the good luck charm.

Me: Oh, I get it. It's the tree. So, why is the teacher wearing the symbol of the tree around his neck? (at this point, I really was starting to prompt them).

K.C.: It's the same shape as the tree and shows us that the teacher has also been there.

P.B.: Yeah, the teacher has already passed the tree test.

J.R. recognized that the "good luck charm", which the teacher wore around his neck, represented the tree that blocked the path of *The Apprentice*. Similarly, K.C. understood that "it's the same shape as the tree and shows us that the teacher has also been there". P.B. followed up on these comments with "yeah, the teacher has already passed the tree test." These comments are significant for a couple of reasons. First, their comments illustrate that all three students were aware of the symbols system and were rearranging the symbolic codes in the text, specifically, the 'lucky charm and the tree', in order to make meaning. Second, each of these students read and write well below their grade levels, based on standardized tests. Third, if these students had not had the opportunity to talk about the text, they might not have been able to make the connections among the charm and the tree as easily and/or as quickly. That is, through exploratory talk (Barnes, 1992) they were able to help each other understand the symbolic codes.

There were several similar instances when the students asked me to rewind or fast forward the video to specific points so that they could show me connections between one point of the story and another. In fact, toward the end of the activity, I literally turned the VCR and the remote control over to them so that they could review the video as they needed to. I recall that I was intrigued by how, in small groups, they searched for specific instances in the story, discussed it among themselves, and then returned to their writing. They understood the principle of recursivity in learning how to read a narrative. That is, looking forward and looking back.

At this point, I decided to capitalize on the students' engagement. With each viewing, the students became more excited and confident about offering their ideas with regards to what they understood in the video. As the students became more confident, I did as well. I decided to investigate whether the students could transfer the idea of 'theme' – or the larger social message embedded in narratives – to *The Apprentice*. We had studied the concept of theme earlier in the year. However, understanding theme has always been a difficult concept for these students, as well as for many mainstream students I taught in the past.

It was at this point I suggested that in groups of three or four, they could view the video at their discretion, looking for symbols and other visual cues that helped them develop the broader social message of the story, a Media Education approach sometimes referred to as 'iconographic analysis'. This reflects Media Education's reliance on semiotics as a way of exploring how and why audiences interpret texts differently.

The students now began to talk about the connotations associated with the images and symbols used in *The Apprentice*. I am using the term symbols here to mean cultural codes as interrelated signs that allow us to explain and understand our world. Some of the symbols, which the students considered significant, and the meanings they associated with them, are listed below:

* Apprentice - a beginner; self
* Teacher - wisdom, experience
* Laughing flowers - pressure; society laughing at *our* mistakes; distraction; frustration

* Cliff - obstacles; people who fell off, and didn't
  get back up to try again
* Hourglass - time is running out
* Two roads - fate; temptation
* Cliff/fall - stupidity; mistakes
* Tree - realization; obstacle
* Sword - strength
* Nose - discouraging; truth; lesson; challenge

By referring to the list of symbols, they developed the following themes:

* We all make mistakes
* Learn from your mistakes
* Don't think you know it all
* Let someone guide you; listen and understand
* Let experience guide you.
* Learning the hard way
* Avoiding obstacles
* Learn first; don't rush

On one hand, I was very pleased by the students' recognition of the connotations of the visual symbols, and their ability to relate these to major themes in the text. It displayed their Literate Behavior of Reading associated with signification.

On the other hand, I recall being a little concerned that I was encouraging them to over-read the video. I cautioned the students about interpreting every item in a visual, or print text, as being a symbol. They more or less ignored my advice, continuously reading and rereading the video, looking for more symbolic elements. I believe their engagement with the text is significant in and of itself.

What I had hoped would last one fifty minute class was now going into its third class. It was obvious to me at this point that I had stumbled onto a real learning experience, for the students and myself. I realized that I needed to get the students to express their ideas about the story as writers.

Me: Alright. Take the rest of the class to write down what the story means to you; like being in the ACE Program, like being an apprentice on your work study.

While some of the students were not pleased with the task of having to write about their ideas, I did not have to coerce or compel many of those who have formerly resisted writing.

A few of the students indicated through talk that they understood the narrative, but had difficulty articulating it in prose. One sixteen year old student, whose ability to read or write was well below that expected at his age and grade level (according to standardized reading tests), decided to refer to the plot model I had taught them several months prior.

THE APPRENTICE

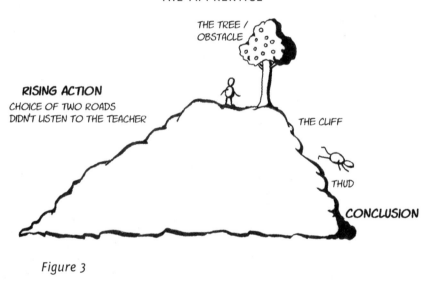

Figure 3

Figure 3 illustrates his way of expressing the narrative using the classical plot model. I was very pleased with his pictorial interpretation of the video. It reinforced my contention that even those students whose literacy levels are well below what we expect in secondary school do possess an understanding of narrative structures.

At this point, several of the students asked if they could watch the video again. Thinking that this was a ploy not to have to write, I grudgingly agreed. As I walked around the classroom, I kept an eye on those in front of the television monitor. Happily, they seemed to be writing as they were reading the video. By the time the fourth period came around, I decided to bring closure to this activity. Keeping in mind that for many of the students, print is something to avoid at all costs, there was some resistance by several students to stop writing. The following are some of the students' insights, as taken from their notebooks:

> "At the end of the story the teacher had a charm of the tree around his neck, which meant that he had already faced the obstacle that the apprentice was going through. Just like our teachers already went through the same obstacles as us, but they let us learn by our mistakes."

> "The teacher knows that the apprentice needs a nose because he's been there before."

> "There are also obstacles in school, not apples or trees, but the temptation to drop out."

> "*The Apprentice* represents the students of the ACE Program because the teachers guide us so we may get experience so we will be able to get over obstacles on our way."

> "We have to make choices just like the apprentice. We have to learn from our mistakes."

> "Thank God this apprentice had a teacher and a tree to get him out of trouble."

> "This class is like the video because the time is running out for us too."

The comments above reveal that M.B. was not the only one in the class who made connections between the characters in the video and their own, personal experiences. Comments such as "just like our teachers already went through the same obstacles as us, but they let us learn by our mistakes", "*The Apprentice* represents the students of the ACE Program because the teachers guide us so we may get experience so we will be able to get over obstacles on our way", and "we have to make choices just like the apprentice" are indicative of the students' literate behavior of constructing subjective meanings based on their prior knowledge and experiences in the ACE Program. Indeed, the students responded affectively, through their personal relationship to the text, and cognitively through their observations. I think this is important, since it demonstrates the importance of relevancy and appropriateness of texts for readers. Earlier, I wrote of the difficulty I had in the beginning of my career getting my students interested in the so called 'high interest-low vocabulary' that books we were reading. *The Apprentice*, on the other hand, was completely relevant to the ACE students.

Chandler (1998) describes the act of reading as, "essentially a sense making activity, consisting of complimentary activities of selection and organization, anticipation and retrospection, the formulation and modification of expectations in the course of the reading process (p. 14)". As it turned out, the ACE students taught me about the complexity and relevancy of this text. I was somewhat humbled by this experience.

Making Personal Connections: *The Apprentice* as an Evolving Autobiography

As I stated earlier, several students were explaining the video by making their own personal connections to it. I have come to understand that students use media texts to mediate their own personal stories. For instance, I noticed that when analyzing media's construction of the world of work or families in television drama and situation comedy programs, the ACE students identify with characters and situations in the programs.

I am going to digress from *The Apprentice* for a moment to pursue this Literate Behavior of making personal connections to texts, by describing the responses of two groups of students to the situation comedies *Roseanne* and *Full House*. I used these two television programs to explore the image of family in the media.

Roseanne is particularly appropriate because of its popularity among my students. Some of the students compared *Roseanne's* fictional family to their own. In fact, as one student remarked, "*Roseanne* is like my family: dysfunctional". Indeed, I have found that some students know *Roseanne's* fictional family as well, and in some cases better, than their own, a rather sad commentary. Each year, that there are several ACE students who come from single parent families, or families in which there are multiple step-mothers or fathers. Some live in group homes.

The students watched the first thirty seconds of the program's opening sequences. The following exchange is typical of the type of dialog that stems from the students' analysis of the opening seconds of *Roseanne*.

Me: Ok, what can you tell me about *Roseanne's* family from the opening?

M.T.: There's junk food on the table.

Me: So?

P.C.: They're poor. He (the son) has a baseball hat and usually rich people don't wear baseball caps.

T. L.: Yeah, and they're eating regular cereal.

Me: What about *Full House?*

S.C.: The way they're dressed— (interrupted).

P.C.: The way they talk isn't real. They don't use slang.

Class: (all at once) Yes they do!

S.C.: (irritated) Yeah, but they don't swear.

P.B.: They're middle class.

Me: How do you know?

S.C.: What they have. Everything looks new. The way they dress. They wake up in the morning and the girls have lipstick on.

Me: What else?

M.B.: They don't argue.

S.C.: The little girl makes me cringe. She's not her age. She's so cute.

J.R.: It's the comments she makes. She puts them in at the right places.

J.T.: She's a wannabe adult.

Now compare the above exchange with the following discussion focusing on the situation comedy, *Full House.*

M.F.: The way (the family) acts is constructed. It's kinda weird that in one day all the stuff happens.

M.B.: Yeah, the date too. They made the date like Cinderella.

J.R.: They didn't show the date. It's over and the weekend
is finished. Then, they're back in school on Monday.

K.G.: The ending is dumb.

M.B.: The principal is not reasonable. He gives everybody two
hours detentions after school. He's the typical principal.
He's been stereotyped.

Me: What image of teens is presented in the program?

S.C.: (cynical) That isn't like real teens! They were too mature!
They had like thirty years' experience. That's not what teens
are like nowadays!

In the above discussions about *Roseanne* and *Full House*, the students
focused on how realistic or unrealistic the families were portrayed. In the
instance of *Roseanne*, some of the students were aware that their ideas of
the images they consume in the media are subjective meanings based on
their own prior experiences and backgrounds and knowledge. This is
evident in comments such as:

M.B.: There's junk food on the table.

Me: So?

P.T.: They're poor. He (the son) has a baseball hat and
usually rich people don't wear baseball caps.

T.R.: Yeah, and they're eating regular cereal.

On one hand, in the excerpts above the students are expressing their
understanding that the images of family in *Roseanne* and *Full House* are
fabrications constructed by the producers for television. That is, the
notion of agency. The students were more accepting of the former, since
'it seemed to be more like their own families'. However, while not saying
it directly, the students were more tolerant and accepting of *Roseanne* as
a fictional family, limited by certain conventions. On the other hand,
many students displayed a real disdain for *Full House*. They were much
more critical of the lack of realism associated with the characters and
plots, even though they were aware that it too was a situation comedy
intended to create humour. This is evident in comments such as:

"The way they talk isn't real. They don't use slang".

"Yeah, but they don't swear".

"They wake up in the morning and the girls have lipstick on".

"The little girl makes me cringe. She's not her age".

"It's the comments she makes. She puts them in at the right places".

"The way (the family) acts is constructed. It's kinda weird that in one day all the stuff happens".

"That isn't like real teens! They were too mature! They had like thirty years' experience. That's not what teens are like nowadays!"

The students were also critical of how time is constructed and how problems or conflicts are resolved:

"They didn't show the date. It's over and the weekend is finished. Then, they're back in school on Monday".

"The ending is dumb".

I believe that some of the students' tolerance for *Roseanne* and rejection of *Full House* is due to their emotional or affective response and connections to the characters.

The point here is that in their analysis of the situation comedies, the students were demonstrating an important aspect of literate behavior critical reading/viewing. That is, they were able to:

1. Distinguish between media's construction of reality and reality.
2. Identify elements of narratives.
3. Identify particular aspects of the characters.

Rosenblatt (1978) remarks:

The reader's attention to the text activates certain elements in his past experience – external reference, internal response – that have become linked with the verbal symbols. The symbols point to these sensations, images, objects, ideas, relationships, with the particular associations or feeling – tones created by his past experiences with them in actual life or literature (p. 11).

Returning to *The Apprentice*, our discussions of the text were in essence dialogs, between the students and I, about what it means to read stories as symbols through which we could better understand ourselves. The symbols provided ways for the students to incorporate into their readings of the text, their own experiences as ACE students – apprentices and as part time workers – as well as their experiences with other mass media texts about the world of work and the family.

The students positioned themselves within the fictional world of the characters in the video. Their reading was more than a shallow retelling of the narrative such as its plot, themes, script, conflict/resolution, symbolism. They responded to the narrative's structure in very specific and personal ways (Masterman, 1985). At the same time, they viewed and identified with the characters on the television monitor, reorganising them in relation to their own experiences and as participants in the viewing process. In Britton's (1975) terms, the ACE students acted in the role of spectator. I argue that acting in the role of spectator is a highly literate behavior indeed.

By appropriating the author's intended message(s) (Willinsky, 1991), and relating it to their own situation, the students reworked the narrative, constructing it as their own personal narratives. In doing so, the students themselves became storytellers. The students unraveled each thread of the story's rhetoric, and spun it into their own autobiographies. By assigning themselves as the main character (student/apprentices in the ACE Program), they retold the story from their particular perspectives and points of view, discovering more about themselves in the process. In Moffett's (1968) words, *The Apprentice* was, for the students, about growth and self knowledge.

The experience reinforced my view regarding the importance of a student's repertoires (McCormick, Waller and Flower, 1992) in the reading and writing process. The students' reading of *The Apprentice* drew from their own experiences, memories (Britton, 1970), and anecdotes, such as the following examples taken from their journals:

1) "The 'flowers' are laughing at the Apprentice, like some people in our school laugh at us in the ACE Program."

2) Students in the ACE Program: "The apprentice represents the students of the ACE Program because the teachers guide us so we may get experience so we will be able to get over obstacles on our way."

3) On the Job Training students: "We have to make choices just like the apprentice. We have to learn from our mistakes."

The Apprentice as a Socio-Cultural Experience

I think that the reading experience of *The Apprentice* was not only a significant lesson in self discovery, but also in allowing each student to discover how others understand the text and themselves.

The ACE students' reading of *The Apprentice* was not an isolated experience. While each student made meaning of the text, sharing their interpretations and representations constituted a collaborative experience. Willinsky (1992) writes that texts serve as foundations for telling and retelling stories, built upon social and cultural experiences. English Language Arts theorists/educators such as Medway (1980) speak of coming to terms with our inner self through talking, reading and writing. The ACE students' interpretations and hypotheses about how they see themselves and how others see them, developed through social interaction, primarily through sharing their ideas with other students in the class. Britton (1970) called this expressive language, and Barnes (1992), referred to this as exploratory talk.

The students and I engaged in a dialog which included negotiation, resistance, consent, verification, and validation. In some ways, this process reminded me of Holdaway's (1979) notion of 'shared reading responses'; reading a story together, pausing from time to time to think about what had been said and written.

This dialogic process was evident in two ways. First, whereas at other times, discussions have led to ridicule some of the comments made by academically and/or socially weaker students, in this instance, the classroom took on an atmosphere of mutual respect. The students seemed engaged with the text. Rather than being ridiculed for their lack of understanding, weaker students actually helped stronger students.

Even those students, who were usually complacent, apathetic, or had difficulty articulating their thoughts, joined in the discussion. Their progressively detailed interpretations developed through a process of building upon each other's insights. Second, Moffett (1968) explains the importance of group discussion in a classroom setting as

> an external social process (in which) each member gradually internalizes as a personal thought process: he begins to think in ways his group talks. Not only does he take unto himself the vocabulary, usage and syntax of others and synthesize new creations out of their various styles, points of view, and attitudes; he also structures his thinking into mental operations resembling the operations of the group interactions. If the group amends, challenges, elaborates, and qualifies together, each member begins to do so alone in his inner speech (p. 46).

The viewing of *The Apprentice* provided a forum for the students to talk openly and purposefully about their lives, their goals, and experiences as apprentices in an open atmosphere which, to the students, was personally purposeful. The students' ideas came from their own stories, real and imagined, and which enabled them to construct an idea of a common culture, making sense of their social world. Shirley Brice Heath (1983) remarks that finding meaning in a text is a social as well as a literary understanding. The interaction among the ACE students and the text demonstrated to me that their reading/viewing was more complex than I had previously thought. It also reinforced for me that the language involved in such social discourse should be included in English Language Arts classrooms, in the same way as are other social discourses.

The ACE students and students like them are often referred to as "reluctant readers". I argue that this is a stereotyped label of at-risk students. While they may be reluctant to read the specific texts demanded of them in schooling, my experience, as I have illustrated here, has been that they are indeed eager readers.

At the beginning of each unit, I ask the students to list popular culture texts, and spin-offs of these, including movies, television programs, videos, songs, toys, games, magazines, and books which are related to the current topic. I am always amazed by the length and magnitude of their lists. For example, in the Fall of 1994, the class was working on the theme of war.

I asked the students to name various television programs/movies, games/toys, songs, magazines/books related to war. I have included below a partial list generated by the students:.

TV Movies	Games/Toys	Songs	Magazines/Books
Platoon	GI Joe	Civil War	Legion
Good Morning Vietnam	Battleship	Wind Beneath	Guns & Ammo
Predator	Contra	One	Untold Story
Top Gun	Commando	War Ensemble	Modern Guns
Casualties	Risk	Angel of Death	Soldier of Fortune
Schindler's List	Turn and Burn	Run to the Hills	Ground Zero

Textual Influences

The Apprentice follows the typical plot formula of introduction, rising action, climax, denouement, and conclusion. The students are accustomed to this pattern, and yet have difficulty with it in print texts. In a way, *The Apprentice* is analogous to a more traditional print, literary work, and I would argue that many of the basic concepts which apply to stories in print apply as well to stories on film and video. The ACE students' engagement with *The Apprentice* was very much the approach and involvement we would hope and expect students in a mainstream English Language Arts class to exercise when occupied with more traditional short stories.

But what was it about *The Apprentice* which solicited such deep insights? What motivated them to 'read' the text as critical viewers, looking beyond common sense meanings and their relationships? What was it that appealed to them about this seemingly nonsensical text in more than just an entertaining way? The students responded to the video beyond a superficial, "Did I enjoy it"? From what is in fact a very simple narrative, the students fashioned a rather complex reading.

The ACE students used the visual and auditory cues, editing and camera work conventions, and formal features of the video, in a manner that led them to ask deeper questions than 'what is the plot, who are the characters and why are they important to the story?'

Some of the characteristics of *The Apprentice* deserve consideration, since they influence the interaction between the ACE students and the text. Audiences react instinctively to images and sounds in films and video symbolically (McKee, 1997). *The Apprentice* audio is limited to nonsensical sound effects, such as garbled dialog and a sound effect signaling an introduction and end to each scene. These offer the reader few clues from which to follow the story. The students read *The Apprentice*, primarily through representations created by its image systems. I have found that many of the students do not have semantic difficulties; in fact, many have quite extensive vocabularies. I think the following exchange best explains their awareness of the characteristics unique to print and non print texts:

M.D.: On TV you can see the characters and how they act and all that.

M.W.: Like a book you have to think. You have to picture what the characters are like. In a movie, it going through before your eyes. You can see what it's like.

B.P.: You can read both (print and TV) the same way.

Me: How do you know when there's an emotional scene?

Class: (all at once) faces, music, close ups, shots.

S.H.: When you watch it, (on tv) you can't feel the mood. You can only feel the action.

Me: You mean the emotional impact?

J.L.: You can understand it more.

Me: Can't you get that in books?

J.L.: Yeah, you get the feelings, but it's not as clear.

Me: What makes the images in movies more emotional?

P.N.: The things they do. The long shots and close ups.

Me: How?

P.N.: 'Cause the extreme close up you can see the person's face; see the all the emotions.

J.S.: Yeah, like Platoon. I can't read the book.

Me: Why?

J.S.: You know, like I'll read the first paragraph and then I can't remember what I read so by the time I finish the book . . . the movie, when I watched it the first time and it seems ok but then I watch it a second time, it's clearer. Like when we watched *The Apprentice*.

J.R.: It's like when you watch a movie and then read the book. They talk about the scene in the book, but in TV they *do* (his emphasis) the scene. The characters and the setting are the same (in the book and tv), but stuff happens, like it's mixed up. This happens, then that happens.

Me: Why is that?

P.N.: Because everyone has their own image.

J.L.: But isn't it the same author?

P.N.: Not always.

S.H.: In texts, I mean books and all that, they have words to create meaning, but in movies they have to use pictures to make it more meaningful.

The students revealed not only a fairly sophisticated understanding of the differences between print, film, and television texts; they also point to considerable metacognitive awareness of their own processing of these texts. Clearly, they are more adept at processing visual rather than print texts. An example of the difficulty some of the students have in following sequences in print texts – and how, after several viewings, they modify their understanding of visual texts by focusing on the symbols, patterns, changes in location and time – is evident in J.S.'s and J.R.'s comments.

J.S.: You know, like I'll read the first paragraph and then I can't remember what I read so by the time I finish the book . . . the movie, when I watched it the first time and it seems ok but then I watch it a second time, it's clearer. Like when we watched *The Apprentice*.

J.R.: It's like when you watch a movie and then read the book. They talk about the scene in the book, but in TV they *do* (his emphasis) the scene. The characters and the setting are the same (in the book and tv), but stuff happens, like it's mixed up. This happens, then that happens.

In reading visual texts such as television and movies, the students draw on their previous media experiences to understand the elements in non-print texts by reading the "faces, music, close ups, shots, the action".

P.N.'s remark that "everyone has their own image" is especially telling of how the ACE students read *The Apprentice*. In *The Apprentice*, they found representations of the main characters and their conflicts parallel to themselves, including the world in which they function (Britton, 1970). They sought out images that provided them with an understanding of the narrative sequences, and which enabled a broader interpretation.

The cartoon characters in the video are neutral and flat. Their main function is to provide the action. As well as the fact that there was no dialog or voice over, the video does not provide the reader with clues to the thoughts and feelings of the characters. Each scene and change of setting is identified by a fade to black, accompanied by an audio signal, best described as a 'bong', as if to say "and then". The students were forced to rely on what Rosenblatt (1968) called "selective attention" to details, looking for clues in the images and actions that would fill in the 'gaps', revealing the story's overall plot and thematic structures. In turn, the students used the clues to support their interpretation of the narrative.

And it was not only singular images that provided the students clues, but also the juxtaposition of the images assisted them in making separations and links. So for instance, the scene in which *The Apprentice* falls to the ground, 'losing his nose' is juxtaposed with the image of the Teacher 'blowing up a nose'. This is reminiscent of Barthes' (1957) notion of "hermeneutic codes" as a set of cues used to understand the narrative. In this way, some of the students were able to single out significant themes, as the story developed:

Me: How does the teacher know to blow up a nose
  for the Apprentice?
K.G.: Because the teacher went through the same thing.
  He knows what is going to happen to the student.
Me: Why was the teacher wearing the tree around his neck?
P.F.: Because the teacher has already been to the tree and knows
  that the student will knock into it also.
M.D.: Yeah Sir, the tree is like the tree of experience or
  something like that.

Here again, the students were revealing the literate behavior of predicting, analysing, and interpreting their responses in the process of reading *The Apprentice*. There is also evidence in the above remarks by the three students that they were able to not only identify specific symbols, such as the nose and the tree, but also to make associations. It is possible that in some instances, such as the one described above, images and symbols that are created by juxtaposition of segments, may be more meaningful for a reader than that created by print. The ACE students had a particular reason for reading the images: to decode the message(s) in the narrative, as well as the cultural codes. Many of their responses to the codes and symbols in *The Apprentice* stemmed from the specific meanings conveyed by the codes. In the class discussions of the multiple readings of *The Apprentice*, the students identified:

* How scenes are linked to each other in relation to the scene before and after (i.e., transition/fluidity).

* Various motifs or themes.

* Specific visual conventions of the medium used to convey meaning, such as fades to black.

* Dominant images and their relevance to the major themes in the narrative.

* Audio cues and their relationship to the development of the narrative.

* Cultural values connoted in the images, such as the flowers laughing.

* Symbolic aspects of the images, such as the tree, the nose, the cliff and connected them to the connotations of the objects.

* How certain groups, such as themselves, can be represented in a text.

The students were quite adept at being able to predict how the story would develop, and in constructing their own textual analysis. They retold the story from a contextual and thematic perspective, indicating evidence of ideological and sociological thinking. *The Apprentice* clearly reveals their understanding that reading is a meaning-making process.

The Oasis

I eventually wrote an article based on our experience with *The Apprentice*, which was published in the *National Film Board*'s magazine entitled, *Animando to Zea* (Rother, 1992). A revised version was also included in a special issue of the *English Quarterly*, Canada's principal English Language Arts journal on Media Education. I have often stated that the ACE students wrote the article; I merely articulated it for them.

Keep in mind that the publication of *The Apprentice* experience was an exciting outcome. For me, it was an acknowledgement of the ACE students' literate behavior. For the ACE students, the articles were a sign of public recognition, something that is usually left for "high achievers".

After reading the article in the *National Film Board* publication, the media center manager for my school board asked if my students would preview a video she was considering buying, entitled *The Oasis*. Naturally, I was more than pleased to accommodate the media center manager, although my motivation was selfish. I was anxious to use *The Oasis* for several reasons. I wanted to see if the experience with *The Apprentice* was more than just a fortunate teachable moment. I also wanted to see if the ACE students could apply the knowledge and ideas they had demonstrated in reading *The Apprentice* to other video texts as well.

The Oasis is a half hour video about a young boy who, in the course of driving through the desert with his parents, embarks on a surrealistic dream to escape his parents' constant arguing. The approach I took reading *The Oasis* with the ACE students was similar to *The Apprentice*, except this time we all had a prior experience to draw on.

The first thing the students noticed was the "letter box" format of the video. Some students had ideas about why the producers used this format. While their notions were technically incorrect, I include the students' ideas here since I think it illustrates their awareness of production techniques, and how audio-visual technology is used to focus a reader/viewers's attention, and how specific visual conventions are used to convey meaning:

* It draws our attention to the center of the screen.

* It's a technical thing, but they left it there for a reason, like to keep our attention on the screen.

* It makes it seem like you're supposed to look at it like a fantasy.

Some of the students thought that the dream-like scenes in the video created a "fantasy mood".

M.S.: It was like a fantasy; a dream.
E.V.: Yeah. His parents were always putting him down. He didn't have any confidence until he imagined those people.
Me: So what might be a theme of the story?
J.L.: Dreams come true.
M.E.: Believe in yourself.
T.P.: If you put your mind to it, you can overcome obstacles.
Me: What were his obstacles"
E.V.: His parents.
Me: What is an oasis?
M.D.: It's different for everyone. A place that . . . something you like to see, like a dream.

As discussed earlier, identification plays a significant role in the ACE students' reading of texts. In *The Apprentice*, many identified with the role of apprentices in their work study. I was especially impressed with E.V.'s understanding of how the oasis was the boy's means of escaping from his parents. E.V. was a very sensitive and insecure sixteen year old. His reading and writing skills were very weak. In general, he had difficulty with much of the class work, such as following directions and completing tasks independently. Consequently, he often became frustrated and gave up easily. However, he quickly identified with the boy in the video.

His statement in the above passage: "his parents were always putting him down / he didn't have any confidence until he imagined those people", makes me feel that E.V. identified with the boy's feelings. Relevance and identification are an important aspect of the literate behavior of reading. At this point, I decided to see if the students could employ symbolization as they did in *The Apprentice*.

The story takes place in a desert. A young boy and his parents are travelling across the desert in a car. In the middle of the desert, the father stops at a roadside diner. The boy strolls outside the diner, coming upon an oasis, inhabited by an ordinary looking man and woman. I asked the students what the significance of the oasis was in the story. One student stated, "the oasis is the kid's hope". His family is arguing all the time, and in the oasis he has hope. Another student described the oasis as "a home away from home".

Throughout story, the boy is struggling to play a saxophone, something that his father does not support. It is only when the boy meets a man in the oasis that he learns how to play the saxophone.

Me: What does the saxophone represent?
E.V.:   The boy's best friend.
M.H.: Escaping from his parents.
P.N.:   Patience.

The students noticed that at the beginning and end of each scene, a turtle appeared moving toward or away from the center of screen, or was present throughout the scene.

Me: Why a turtle?
J.R.: It's a signpost saying welcome to your dream It was like an entrance or an exit sign.
K.G.: It's his guardian angel.
M.S.: It leads him to peace.
E.V.: Answers to problems come slow, and the turtle is slow.
Me: Why a desert?
M.H.: There are no mirages in cities.
P.N.: And it's a dream.
E.V.: In a desert, no one can hear him. He can play his saxophone.

As was the case in *The Apprentice*, some of the students were able to exhibit their ability to understand that grammar and syntax of symbols systems mean different things for different people. J.R.'s remark that the turtle is "a sign post saying welcome to your dream / it was like an entrance or an exit sign" is a good example of this aspect of literate behavior.

In the following scene, I provide a more detailed example of how their reading of a full-length, animated cartoon program, in which the students, although unaware, used concepts such as signs, signification, denotation, and connotation to create meaning. The example shows that the ACE students' textual analysis can be considered in the broader discipline called semiotics.

Teenage Mutant Ninja Turtles

I like to incorporate popular culture texts in my teaching for several reasons. First, popular texts are a common experience for students. Spenser (1986) refers to texts such as those found in mainstream television as sites of emergent literacies, which are not available in schools. Second, popular media texts can act as a leveler in the sense it enables students, at varying literacy levels, to be a part of, and indeed, contribute to the learning experience in English Language Arts. Third, it draws from the students' prior experience. Fourth, such texts are, for students, reflections of their values, beliefs, knowledge, and assumptions. Finally, as Moffett (1968) points out, I see a connection among primary texts and the everyday life experiences of students.

The text, *Teenage Mutant Ninja Turtles: The Epic Begins*, is a full-length seventy-two-minute, animated, video version of what was in the early nineties a popular television series, cartoon program. Because the students were familiar with the myth behind *Teenage Mutant Ninja Turtles*, I stopped the video at the end of the opening sequence in order to find out how much prior knowledge the ACE students have of *Teenage Ninja Mutant Turtles*. In this excerpt, some of the students contrasted the everyday idea of a turtle with the image created in the media of the Ninja culture:

Me: Do you consider the Turtles monsters?

D.C.: Well Sir, no. Turtles are slow and dull. They look weak.

G.S.: Ya, Ninja's are powerful, fast and slick. They control their
bodies. That's why they chose them as good guys.
It's not like real turtles.

Me: What does mutant mean?

D.S.: No, I think mutant means kind of an amphibian or um....

G.S.: I think it means change.

J.B.: (forcefully) Mutant means change or transformation.

Me: What does Ninja mean?

D.S.: (excitedly) Ninja means a kind of Karate.
The most dangerous thing of Karate.

Teenage Mutant Ninja Turtles: The Epic Begins, was part of an introduction to a "cultural studies" unit I do every alternate year as part of the ACE Program. The unit I developed has the following steps:

* An introduction to popular culture
* A discussion of what makes a popular text popular
* A "close reading" of a popular culture text
* A multi-media advertising campaign for a product
  that they have developed

While the students get to develop a popular text of their own, initially I invoke teacher privilege in choosing a text to demonstrate how to do a close reading. I chose *Teenage Mutant Ninja Turtles* for several reasons, some academic, others more esoteric. These reasons were:

* The programs turned out to be semiotically more
  advanced than I had anticipated, and I became hooked
  on their analysis.

* My interest in Saturday morning cartoons within the
  context of mythology and semiotics, triggered an idea of
  how I might, within the context of the cultural studies unit,
  introduce the ACE students to basic formulaic patterns,
  genre, plot, and character, in popular texts.

Reading the Teenage Ninja Mutant Turtles

The ACE students' reading of *Teenage Mutant Ninja Turtles: The Epic Begins*, illustrates how, as readers/users of popular texts, they were able to "read" the text at a rather sophisticated level, based on prior knowledge learned in the ACE Program.

Their reading involved analysing the:

* Denotative levels of the text.
* Connotative levels of the text, including format, genre, narrative closure
* The ideological structures of the text (McCormick, Waller & Flower, 1992).

Most of the students had no problem providing a detailed synopsis of the myth behind the Turtles. I assumed their ease in recounting the narrative was due to their familiarity from watching the television program, a "Saturday morning cartoon". Several of the students seemed embarrassed to admit that they indeed had watched the cartoon, and actually enjoyed it. More importantly, one of the students commented that "all cartoons start the same way. Ninjas is like Robocop". His comments point to his understanding of the conventions of the text by making specific references to another text that employed the same conventions.

The opening of Teenage Mutant Ninja Turtles, lasting approximately five minutes – including theme song – relies heavily on a series of fast moving images. The purpose of the opening sequence is to introduce the viewer to the:

1) overall form of the text;

2) the Turtles' "mythical transformation" into humanoid form;

3) each of the protagonists, including the four Turtles, their mentor, Splinter, a rat, transformed from a human, and the antagonist, Shredder, who maintains human form;

4) the Turtles, as archetype heroes, journey on a "mythical quest" to find an antidote that will return their mentor to human form. In the process, the heroes protect and save themselves and their human friends from succumbing to the powers of their archenemy Shredder. The remainder of the narrative is a series of redundant s dominated by battles between good and evil, characterising the underlying theme of danger and a return to safety, found in similar fantasies.

In some ways, the narrative's formula is reminiscent of the classical myth, in which the main characters' orderly world is upset, leading to a quest that will restore the equilibrium. Even the title prepares us for the narrative. For instance, words like "epic" and "ninjas" can be read as a metonym for the narrative's spiritual and mythical theme, based in tradition and history. Similarly, "mutant" adds to the foreboding theme concerning the dangers of nuclear technology.

While the tone of the narrative is, by definition, exaggerated. and thus humorous to children and teens, it also brings together certain polar elements (Hodge & Tripp, 1986; Propp, 1968) that I will expand on later: for instance, animal and human, young and old, protagonist and villain, ancient and modern, tradition and technology.

A Comparison of My Close Reading of *Teenage Mutant Ninja Turtles* with the ACE Students'

The Narrative Structure

The narrative's characters, images, themes, events, and symbols make it an archetypal myth. Analysing the sequence of events that form the plot – syntagmatic analysis (Hodge and Tripp, 1986) – and using Propp's (1968) notations – **PR** - *pursuit,* **H** - *struggle* and **Rs** - *rescue* – I developed the following diagram to illustrate the students' and my comparative analysis of the narrative's overall structure. *Figure 4* illustrates my semiotic reading.

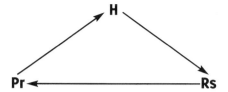

Figure 4

I read the narrative of the video as a series of closed, reoccurring mini-adventures that advance the story. Each of these follows a pattern of pursuit, followed by a conflict, ending in a rescue by the Turtles. What makes each mini-adventure novel is the introduction of new characters, good and evil. Each mini-adventure was in some ways unique, each standing alone, but still part of the overall structure of the narrative.

The students' reading of the plot's structure was continuous and open, rather than closed (*see Figure 5*). In their words, the plot centered on "chase and search" functions, instead of pursuit and rescue. Several of the students referred to other programs, both live and animated, that employ the same type of structure, illustrating their awareness of how one text can be understood through the experience of another:

D.C.: It's about saving the world.

J.B.: Yeah, the bad guys want to capture the power of the earth. The action keeps the series going.

The students' view of the narrative is illustrated in *Figure 5* below.

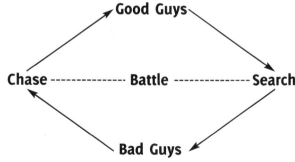

Figure 5

They agreed with me that there was not really a conclusion; that the video was a spin off, the purpose of which was to extend the television series and the myth. That is, the video was in fact a two-hour commercial, the purpose of which was to entice viewers to watch the weekly version.

Structural Patterns of Oppositions: The Characters

The analysis developed above provided both the plot's structure, as well as mapped the pattern of structural oppositions (Hodge & Tripp, 1986; Lévi-Strauss, 1976). Fiske and Hartley (1978) described these as vertical sets of opposites. Much of the students' and my analysis of binary, central polar oppositions were developed from the opening images in the first five minutes of the video.

Using the polar oppositions, central and paired oppositions (Hodge and Tripp, 1986), I developed what I will call the cultural oppositions as shown in *Figure 6*.

MY CULTURAL OPPOSITIONS	Turtles	Shredder
Polar Oppositions	Nature Man Human Animal	Culture Technology Animal Human
Central Oppositions	Man Male/Female	Technology Male
Paired Oppositions	Primary Colours Slang High Pitch Good Conformists Romantic	Tones Contemporary Low Pitch Evil Non-conformists Mechanistic

Figure 6

The ACE Students' Cultural Oppositions

As is typical of all myths, the Turtles and the villains take on supernatural dimensions. They are both human and animal, as products of nature. At the same time, they are characterized by their appearance and weaponry as products of man's technological accomplishments and mismanagement. In Levis Strauss' (1976) words, the Turtles and their enemies are "segregated outside the natural environment of which [they are] morally as well as physically an inseparable part" (p. 284).

The ACE students' cultural oppositions are illustrated in *Figure 7*.

ACE STUDENTS' CULTURAL OPPOSITIONS	
Ninja Turtles & Allies	**Shredder & Accomplices**
Hip	Normal
Male	Male
Teenagers	Older
Bright Colors	Dark Colours
Good Guys	Bad Guys
Defenders	Villians

Figure 7

The real difference between the students' analysis and mine was not in the construction of the oppositions, but rather in the manner in which the students constructed them. That is, they analyzed the characters through their physical, descriptive attributes, as well as their roles.

Almost all of the discussion was dominated by the boys in the class. Even when it came to discussing April, the only female character in the narrative, the males referred to her as an "agent of the Turtles". Obviously, the ACE students considered that both the video and the television series were aimed at a male audience.

Setting

Having explored how the students understood the characters, we turned our attention to the setting of the story.

> **Me**: Why underground?
> **D.C.**: If everybody was above ground, it would be like norm. It's like Beauty and the Beast.
> **Me**: What's the difference between above ground and below ground?
> **D.C.**: Below ground is lower than civilisation. Above ground is everybody is there.

The narrative takes place both above and below ground. The Turtles and their leader, Splinter, reside in a subterranean world, the sewers under the city. According to the students, the Turtles' "hide-out" was in the sewer to protect them from their adversaries, as well as from man's "natural habit of disturbing or destroying anything abnormal". The students also suggested that below ground also makes for "a better grandstand entry". The students' analysis of the video is illustrated below:

Above Ground	Below Ground
Heroes return	Hidden
Danger	Protection
Evil	Safe
Life	Peace

The students' description of the setting more or less matched my own. It brought to my mind notions of "dystopia". That is, they grasped the idea that the world above ground was in constant turmoil.

As a result of comparing and contrasting my semiotic analysis and that of my students, I now realize how the ACE students' analysis of the video process moved from focusing on the content of the narrative to understanding its structure. I was thus able to get at some of the following complex literate behaviors of these students.

Reading as a Risk-Taking Experience

In the first few months of the ACE program, many students are hesitant to join in classroom dialog. I think this is a coping skill that they have developed from their previous class experiences. Using popular texts as a common experience has been a great asset in getting them to participate in literary discussions. During the course of discussing the texts, the students were confident enough to provide ideas that they had not fully worked out, but were willing to offer to others in the class to develop. This often manifested itself as seemingly disruptive behavior. Students called out their thoughts, interrupted one another, etc.

In the process of dialoguing about popular texts, I have learned not to regard the ACE students' argumentative and general disorderly behavior as a problem to be stifled, although I must admit it does stretch my patience. Rather, I consider their behavior a positive reaction to literacy experiences, rare occurrences for at-risk students, both at home and in school. It is these experiences that recruit students, such as the ACE students, into membership in what Frank Smith (1988) called the 'literacy club'. From their own retellings of *The Apprentice, The Oasis* and the *Teenage Mutant Ninja Turtles*, it was clear to me that the ACE students:

* Had an understanding of basic narrative structures.
  I was surprised how well the students were able to relate
  the video to other television programs and genres, live
  and animated.

* Relied on already learned Media Literacy skills in their
  attempt to understand the symbolic elements created
  by the visual and audio codes operating together and
  separately in the video message.

* Based on the video, the students were able to construct
  a thematic perspective of the cartoon series as a whole.

* Developed, from simple narrative elements, complex sets
  of oppositions.

* Recognized how the producers appealed to younger
audiences through the non-realistic elements.

Reading for Pleasure

It is important to remember that, except for the *Teenage Mutant Ninja Turtles*, the choice of texts was not mine, nor the students, but rather the result of requests from my colleagues. Also, the students struggled with their interpretations, not from the sense of correctness according to my standards, but from their own need to make sense of the narratives. This suggests to me that if students are to enjoy literary experiences, they don't necessarily have to "like" the material. Rather, enjoyment comes with being able to find a way of encountering texts which enables all readers to join in the act of reading.

Perhaps Rosenblatt's (1968) idea of readers of texts as 'performers' who derive pleasure in a text merely by making meaning is a fitting analogy to describe the ACE students' involvement in the readings. Pleasure is an aspect which I believe is often overlooked in classroom encounters with literature. It is thus a dimension of literate behavior. Medway (1980) believes that it is through the pleasure of a text, rather than lessons about texts, that students may be motivated to engage with reading and writing.

The enthusiasm and assertiveness that many of the ACE students demonstrated in the act of reading the videos is difficult to express in prose. It seemed to me that they got "lost" in reading, interpreting and discussing the texts in the same way that others get lost reading a book.

Their experience with popular texts, such as the Ninja Turtles, counters the idea that at-risk students are disinterested in literature. My students learned, as David Lusted (1991) notes, that reading narratives is about picking apart story-telling, both our own and that of others, and in the process finding the experience intrinsically rewarding. Making experiences with literature enjoyable is also a vital role of English Language Arts teachers.

The Apprentice, The Oasis, and *Teenage Ninja Mutant Turtles* illustrate the ACE students' literate behavior in the act of reading media texts. Their responses to the texts can be judged in much the same way that we judge students' responses to traditional forms of literature (books) in mainstream English Language Arts classrooms.

Story Elements

It is clear that the ACE students were aware of the following story elements and their functions in each of the texts discussed:

* characters
* plot
* setting
* mood
* structure
* symbolisation
* representation
* theme

The students used and compared these elements to interpret and construct their meanings of *The Apprentice*, *The Oasis*, and *Teenage Mutant Ninja Turtles*.

The Interpretation Process

The ability to interpret is as basic to non-print texts as it is to print, and a strong indicator of literate behavior. For the ACE students, interpretation came about through 'purposeful talk' (Barnes, 1992). In the process of interpretation, the ACE students asked questions of each other and myself in order to clarify personal ideas. There were few instances when the students disrupted the classroom dialogs by disagreeing with each other. They appreciated each other's contributions to the interpretive development of the narratives.

During the course of reading the texts, they sometimes called out their predictions of what would occur next, as well as implied meanings not outwardly apparent in the texts. In fact, I was pleased that, for the most part, the students were able to follow the story sequence, something which I found they had difficulty doing in traditional print texts. I was especially impressed by their ability to identify the various structural levels, as in their interpretation of *Teenage Mutant Ninja Turtles*. I think that a lot of this is a result of their keen engagement with the texts.

The Literate Behavior of Writing

Thus far, I have focused the discussion of the ACE students' literate behavior in the process of "reading". That is, making meaning, through the language of audio visual media texts. As well, I have attempted to make links to what we, as English Language Arts teachers, require of students when they are asked to make sense of more traditional literary texts.

But textual analysis is only one side of the same coin. Many media educators/theorists (Buckingham & Sefton Green, 1994; Masterman, 1985) have argued that practical work, also referred to as production, is vital to learning about the media. Borrowing from *The Media Files* (Emery, et al., 1995), as well as from Buckingham (1994), I see "writing media" as an active and discursive social construction of texts for real and imagined audiences.

I considered the ACE students' media productions as extensions of writing in the traditional sense. For instance, once the students completed their treatments, storyboards, and scripts, I provided them with a video camera and asked them to "write their essays" rather than "shoot their productions". Having shot their raw footage, the students then "edit and revise and/or expand" their productions, much like what we ask students to do with their print essays. As you read through the following sections, you will note how the ACE students approached their media projects' writing, drafting, editing, and talking in similar fashion to the way students approach writing print in an English language Arts classroom.

In this section, I describe the students' literate behavior as it is manifested in their productions. I will describe how, "doing" media projects provided them with opportunities to use language skills in realistic ways – planning, organising, revising, editing – and in ways that we traditionally consider oral and written development: rehearsing, drafting, revisioning, publishing.

Marketing a Popular Culture Product:
A Simulation in Enterpreneurship

Marketing A Popular Culture Product: A Simulation in Entrepreneurship
was a multi media, cross-curricular project. In groups of three or four,
ACE students were required to develop a popular culture product,
adapted from something in existence or something new, and aimed at a
specific audience. Group members assumed one of the following roles:
media producers, researchers, text editors, video editors, artists, talent.
The students were provided with a "fictional" amount of money as a
working budget from which to finance the development of a prototype,
packaging, and a multi-media advertising campaign, such as television,
radio, and print, for their product.

The ACE Students' Knowledge of
Media Language and Concepts

In this section, I will describe the students' knowledge of specific aspects
of media industries, including advertising, audience research, economics,
and the processes by which media and popular culture products are
produced and distributed. As well, I will provide examples of their
awareness of the form and conventions associated with media texts
produced by media industries.

Advertising

Part of the Marketing Project required the ACE students to produce
a print advertisement such as a newspaper or magazine ad, and a thirty
second television and radio commercial. I started the advertising section
of the project by reviewing the communication model. The model that I
presented to the students is a set of relationships among a sender, a
receiver, and a message, bound by a purpose; all communication should
involve feedback, where the receiver of the message becomes the sender
of information to indicate whether or not the message has been received
and understood. What follows evolved from the students' discussion of
the communication model:

S.C.: Communication is about getting a message across.

Me: Right, communication is also about sharing ideas.

J.D.: Yeah, passing on information, but you've got to be able to understand the information.

M.D.: Yeah, what's the use of receiving information if you don't understand it? You have to be able to take some kind of action.

J.R. and M.D. demonstrated their knowledge of the communication model as a set of relations among sender, receiver, and message (Moffett and Wagner, 1976), as well as a "sense of audience". This is illustrated in their comments that, "you've got to be able to understand the information" and "what's the use of receiving information if you don't understand it? You have to be able to take some kind of action". M.D. was aware that in order to be sure that a message not only reached the intended audience, but also that the audience understood it, required some sort of action. That is, M.D. realized that if the advertisement was successful, it meant that those who saw it purchased the product advertised. Without knowing it, M.D. was referring to the formula known in the advertising industry as AIDA: attention, interest, desire, and action. Action here refers to the purchase of a product, or in the case of a public service announcement, acceptance of an idea.

Having presented the model, the students participated in several activities focusing on how advertisements are developed for specific audiences.

Me: How do advertisers create appeal?

J.L.: They attract us. They use tricks to create a desire.

Me: Like fantasy. Can you give me some examples?

M.H.: Like Bounty and the desert island.

Me: How about promises?

P.F.: Weight watchers.

Me: Sex.

E.V.: Good looking guys and girls. Club Med have that.

Me: Health.

J.S.: ParticipACTION.

Me: Acceptance.

K.B.: Clearasil.

In the above exchange, the students were able to display the literate behavior of constructing subjective meanings based on their prior knowledge. In this example, they linked their previous social and cultural knowledge of stereotypical images of the ideal man and woman, with an awareness of how advertisements use words and images to play into the desire to live up to theses images.

Since this was an initial introduction to advertising appeals, and I had not previously provided examples or models, I was surprised by how quickly the students were able to make the connections among specific advertising appeals and specific products. For instance, the students were quick to make the connection that the Weight Watchers advertisement appealed to the notion of making promises. I think this illustrates their understanding of how media language takes advantages of connotations.

Also, the students were aware of the notion of agency in advertising: the idea that there are individuals behind the advertisements whose motivation is to manipulate a viewer.

While activities such as the one described above, provided the students with an awareness of how advertisers reach an audience, it was during producing their own commercials that they began to truly understand the importance of making a message clear to the audience. Actual hands-on experiences using various media technology – video cameras, video editing, audio mixer – demystified how media can be used to attract an audience to a product.

One group of boys created a thirty-second television commercial for their board game, *GODZ and DEMONS*, appropriated from *Dungeons & Dragons*. According to these students, the appeals they used were:

Fantasy: We are in the past, with knights and dragons
    and demons.
Power: The game is about power, and who will be the
    strongest to win the war.

I was really excited about the depth of involvement this group of students displayed in creating the commercial for *GODZ and DEMONS*. The day of shooting, they came to school with various costumes and props, some borrowed from the school's drama department, and some that they themselves created.

Indeed, the boys' commercial was much more than a pitch for their product. It was a story that they themselves conceived of, and which they communicated through drama. Drama is a natural part of media production, but is often overlooked in high school Media Education programs. This is somewhat ironic, since drama involves turning ideas into spoken words and actions. Engaging in drama enabled the boys who produced *GODZ and DEMONS* for their media project to use language for an authentic purpose. They wrote for a real audience, in this instance their classmates, a target audience, and myself. It also developed their understanding of how language can be used in various forms and functions. That is, the transactional, poetic, expressive (Britton, 1970). It also provided the students with an opportunity for developing collaborative skills, as well as learning about plot and characterization.

Interestingly, some of the boys who developed *GODZ and DEMONS* seldom openly volunteered to participate in classroom dialog or in writing activities. I have often thought that such students possess poor self-concept and lack confidence, and so choose to become invisible in class through non-participation. And yet, here they were engrossed in parody, speech, expression, and role play, the opposite of non-participation.

One aspect of all of the students' work which may not be apparent here is that they produced many drafts of their work, according to our discussions: revising, editing, and revising again. Significantly, they rarely complained about having to revise their work. In fact, many of them took pride in the number of drafts they produced. That is, they felt a sense of accomplishment. This in itself is significant when we consider that writing was something that most of the ACE students greatly disliked, and in some cases, feared.

Teaching about Audiences and Media Consumption Habits

Teaching about audiences provides students with knowledge about the influences and impact of media on individuals and society as a whole. The ACE media projects required the students to conduct audience research. This included investigating audiences' media preferences, consumption habits, program scheduling, censorship, product placement, ratings and the relationship of these to the economics of media industries.

I was not surprised by the students' knowledge of the various local radio stations and their audiences. Nor was I surprised that their preferences of musical genres ranged from heavy metal to western to classical music. However, I did not expect that some of them were aware of such a diversity of radio stations. In fact, in researching the cost of advertising on the radio, part of the requirements of the multi media advertising campaign, J.S. telephoned and spoke to the station manager of Vermont Public Radio. Another radio station which I did not expect the students to have knowledge of, or an interest in, was McGill University's radio station, CKUT. Yet some of the students decided to place their ads on CKUT, because they thought that their products might appeal to the "college crowd".

From time to time, I asked the students to put what they had learned in their projects into practical application. This could be in the form of a letter. T.P.'s letter below demonstrated her knowledge of the type of music that the station played and what it did not play. More importantly, she indicated an awareness of some of the potential pitfalls and benefits of appealing to a wider audience:

Dear CHOM:

I would like to congratulate you on you a very good radio station. I decided to write to you to give you a couple of suggestions to make your station better. I know quite a few people that listen to CHOM and like it very much. But in a way you are catering to one group of people. A lot of your listeners are teenagers and a lot of teens listen to heavy metal music. I've noticed that your radio station doesn't play any heavy metal. A lot more people would tune in if that sort of music was played. I know that you would lose some listeners but you would gain more than you would lost. Please take this into consideration. Thank you for your time.

Yours Truly,
a dedicated CHOM listener,

T.P.

The following description of one group's marketing project illustrates the ACE students' knowledge of pitching a product to a specific target audience:

Docsy Cool Dude
Below is a description of this groups' product.

We are using as a Cabbage Patch Kid, and turning it into a skin head doll. Our doll will be wearing: a peace sign, Doc shoes, bush jacket, earing going from ear to the nose, tatoo, ripped jeans, a lot of chains. The doll is about 1 foot high.

As pointed out previously, the students' description of the doll demonstrated their literate behavior of connecting their previous social and cultural knowledge with specific text, conventions, genres of media products. They also demonstrated that particular products are developed with very specific demographic information in mind (i.e., gender, socio-economic status, and age). It seems that they have also taken into account the amount that parents would be willing to pay for their product as demonstrated in the following comment:

Our doll is aimed at ages 8 and up. It is for both male and female, and it is for lower class and middle class. Our doll will cost $34.99 + tax.

Since we had studied demographics related to audience research in previous projects, I was pleased to see that the students had transferred their knowledge to this project as well. I was especially pleased that this particular group had also recognized the psychology involved in reaching their target audience. This is an issue we had talked about, but which I did not sense had really sunk in. Indeed, I am not sure that I really made an effort to emphasise the "psychological aspects" of audience research. Why didn't I? Is it possible that I assumed that none of the ACE students were capable of understanding such concepts? If I did, it was a reminder to me that I still possessed some of my own prejudices about the abilities of at-risk students. In any event, the students' description of their target audience's psychology proved once again that I had underestimated their literate abilities, in this case around complex issues related to media industries, including marketing and distribution:

> Our doll will be popular for many reasons. A lot of younger kids want to be like older sisters or brothers or even teenagers they see on the street. They want to be older. Basically they look up to skin heads, so they would want this doll, it is an image of them. It's like their sign, their identity.

The students here recognized the process of identification, and the importance of representation in social differentiation and cultural identity. The analysis of the target audience and their motives for wanting the doll are quite sophisticated for so-called at-risk students. The articulation of the analysis is remarkably coherent and persuasive. Also, I would like to think that their reference to the term "sign", is a consequence of the textual analysis work (i.e., denotation/connotation), done previously.

The Economics of Media Industries

M.D., T.P., W.A., and W.L. comprised a very "active" group. M.D. and T.P. were especially vocal and opinionated. They were also very productive. Their idea for a Popular Culture Product was "Musical Carpets" which, when stepped on, played the music of different groups. These students produced prototypes of two of their favorite rock groups.

Another requirement of the Marketing Project is the development of a business plan, including budget, showing expected expenditures for such things as producing a prototype, packaging, advertising on television, radio and print media, as well as profit margins. The students' discussion below illustrates their awareness of the economic determinants of the media industry.

> **M.D.:** OK, we have to air our commercial three times a day . . .
> **T.P.:** We don't have enough money for three times a day!
> **M.D.:** (emphatically) Yes we do! OK . . . (figuring costs)
>   it's costing . . . 87 . . . 95
> **W.L.:** So we don't have so much.

M.D.: Yes we do. We cut it out of our profit. Where's our profit taker?

W.L.: Are you getting this down?

M.D.: We have $60 000 profit, so we'll take out $20 000..

T.P.: OK, M. I'm going to copy this all over again.

M.D.: (ignoring T.P.) OK, we take out $21,000.

T.P.: How much do we have left?

W.L.: I hate money!

M.D.: OK. $22,000 ... we have $66 000, plus $22 000 equals (figuring on calculator) ... 03588.

I was surprised how immersed the students became in their projects. In their regular math class, many of the ACE students, including most in this group, showed little interest in the contextless expectations of addition, subtraction, multiplication, and division, or even of simulated problems in their textbooks. However, the above exchange continued for at least an hour, during which time there was a considerable amount of calculations, in particular by M.D. The dialog also included:

* Needed capital for producing the carpets and marketing.
* The cost of advertising three times per day, for three weeks on television and radio, during prime time on Music Plus and YTV .
* The cost of advertising in magazines, and comparisons of texts among different media.
* Comparisons of the costs in order to scrutinize which medium to advertise in.

In fact, the students became so involved in their "financial" discussions that they ignored the bell at the end of class, a rare occurrence.

Another significant and humorous anecdote involving M.D. and those in his group occurred toward the end of this project. In conducting market research for the *Musical Carpet*, the ACE designers telephoned a well-known local record distributor to see whether they might be interested in their product. Below is an abbreviated account of the telephone conversation:

M.D.: (anxiously) My name is M. I represent (each group was referred to by a factious company name, which the students invented). We have a prototype of a product you may be interested in. (Mike went on to describe their product).

Distributor: That sounds interesting. Why don't you meet with us, and we can discuss it further.

M.D.: (extreme nervousness) Look, we're just a bunch of high school students! (hangs up).

What is significant is what followed immediately after the above telephone exchange. The students in M.D.'s group were at first unsure what to make of the conversation; was the man on the other end of the phone serious about wanting to see their product, or was he being condescending? Back in the classroom, some of the group members jokingly scolded M.D. for not taking the man's offer to bring the *Musical Carpet* to his office for consideration. The broader outcome of this event was that the students realized that their ideas had merit. It provided them with a temporary "ego boost". The positive experience transferred into subsequent projects. Furthermore, it illustrates an important point about their literate behavior and their abilities as communicators. Part of the success of the telephone conversation lay in the students' effective articulation of the nature of their product to the company representative. As teachers, we often compliment students on a text they have written: a story, a composition, an essay. In a similar way, the man's offer to see the carpet was to the students like having someone other than a teacher compliment their text.

A Socio-Cultural Media Education Project: Gender and Minority Groups in the Media, the Workplace, and Society

The *Images of Gender and Minority Groups in the Media and the Workplace Project* was an attempt to have the students conduct socio-cultural research. The actual project was the culmination of two weeks of in class dialoguing, reading, viewing, and writing about the media's construction of men and women, and minority groups.

I explained to the students that there were several aims for the project. These were to: 1) compare/contrast the media's images as we discussed in class; 2) explore their own question about gender or minority groups; and 3) get to know themselves better. I explained that they were to work in teams, and that each team was to develop its own question based on either gender or minority issues related to the images created in our discussions.

The Report: Purpose, Audience, and Conventions

The teams presented a written dossier to me. The dossiers contained: a title page, an introduction stating what they wanted to investigate, and why, a copy of a multiple choice questionnaire, a copy of the results of the questionnaire presented in table or graph form, and an analysis and explanation of the results. Each team wrote a synthesis of the important information they discovered from the raw data into a written text. Thank you letters to people interviewed were also included. Some students included a video tape of their interviews and/or a mini documentary of their project. Evaluation was based on the dossier, a written synthesis using the data they collected, an oral presentation, and team work.

The project conducted by M.E., J.F., C.A., and P.M. was an example of a Gender Project. They described their focus for investigation this way:

> In our group we will find out about which jobs women are most rejected from and the reasons for that. We will interview three people, preferably company bosses in an executive position. We will also ask women workers their good and bad points, and what they are.

Their project included several types of writing, aimed at different audiences, word processing, charts, and statistics. I think this is a good example of what Britton (1970) was referring to when he spoke of using different forms of writing for different audiences, which I see as an indication of the students' literate behavior of writing. Furthermore, many students were able to demonstrate a considerable competence in attending to conventions of print discourse: form, paragraphing, sentence structure, and surface features of the language: areas which for whatever reason had to be dragged out of them in formal essay writing.

While many of the students have wide knowledge and opinions on how race and gender are represented in the media, in general they are not forthcoming in discussions that take place in a classroom setting. The outcome of the media projects, in which the students explore these two topics, had a tendency to motivate them to voice their opinions in both informal discussions with peers and in formal discussions in the class, as expressed in their comments below:

> Before I did not even think of gender or minorities. I knew there were, but I did not really look at it the way I do now. I still don't really understand gender, but I really understand minorities. I see them everywhere, like at school, workplace, and where I hang out. Doing our minority project, Jason and I have discovered a lot of little things that people usually see.

> Like sexism, I didn't know much about it, but I did a project on it so now . . . I interviewed doctors and stuff and getting opinions from everybody else, so like I involved my school related activities.

> I did learn quite a bit, and having to do a project on Gender helped me understand the importance of understanding the problems of Gender and Minorities in our society. I've become more aware so now I tell others.

Comments such as the ones above illustrate many of the ACE students' awareness of the social, cultural, and ideological issues in the media they consume, after working on projects. At the end of the Gender and Minorities Project, one student wrote in her journal:

> I find that I have become aware of gender and minority issue in TV and movies. Whenever people start talking about such things I get antsy, and speak my mind.

Another girl wrote:

> I find that women in television and movies are stereotyped (and have lot of sexism). To prove this theory in the past I have done projects, surveys, and interviews. The facts that I got was that a lot of men think that women should stay home barefoot and pregnant.

Others have said that women should not be in high authority because they are too soft, weak, or too understanding to take anything seriously. I find myself that there are now more women in authority but still not enough.

Watching television, movies and rock videos have got my family and I into a lot of arguments. It could have been over the easiest, agreeable issue, but they just don't understand. Take for instance sexism or such, that isn't clearly visible unless you have an open mind about issues like these.

The student's remark, that "sexism isn't clearly visible unless you have an open mind" is interesting. She realized that she was constructing her own, subjective meanings of the images she was viewing. I think this is, in part, is the result of what she learned from a practical exercise we did in class, in which the students are asked to consider possible opposition messages in magazine ads. As a follow up, using the same magazine advertisement, the students produced an "oppositional" text (Fiske, 1982).

ACE Student Learning from Media Projects

Outcomes of the ACE students' learning, resulting from the media projects, were not always immediate. Perhaps some of the most personally satisfying comments I get from my students are in letters from graduates of the ACE program:

> And when I was in the ACE Program we did a hell of a lot of papers on TV and the media. It's good in a way because now when I watch an ad on TV I break it down in my head.

and

> I see things much differently since I've worked with the media, and I've only learned a little. I seem to have learned very much. With books and magazines I get to reading articles, and now I pick up more than I would normally have. In TV and movies some parts in the shots they take, and I critique them and think of what kind of shot I would have taken.

Sometimes, this new awareness can lead to awkward situations in the homes of ACE students'. Parents have told me that their once, uncommunicative son/daughters, are constantly commenting on what they are watching, sometimes making family viewing difficult, as expressed by one of the students:

I have arguments with my little brother and my mother about almost all the t.v. shows because single and career women are the big thing in the nineties (*Grace Under Fire*). Me and my brother always argue about that show and also *Murphy Brown*. Single mothers in the workforce is the new thing in the 90s. I always win the battle about these topics because I learned a lot about them.

Another student wrote:

Covert commercials are the biggest issue in my house. I can't watch anything without noticing a covert commercial. It gets on my parents' nerves, so they can't say I don't listen and learn.

One student seemed to have a solution to keeping peace in her family:

Me and my family we don't usually discuss or argue. My parents got their t.v and I got mine, so we can't really argue.

Developing Conceptual Behaviors

An important element of literate behavior is the ability to form bridges between one's prior knowledge and new areas of understanding in the process of reading and/or writing a media text. In the comment below, the student made reference to her awareness that she had heard certain words in what she was viewing on television, and, as a result of the media projects had come to realize their meaning:

It all changed when we started all the projects. I started to hear more words on t.v. that we used in class and I would of never known these words or understood the meaning of the topic. I noticed more and more as I went along every project that I learned more and more. Gender and minorities is a problem but still I learned a lot.

Being aware of and being able to use specific visual conventions, such as camera shots, angles, and movement to convey meaning is an important aspect of the Literate Behavior of Writing. I am always delighted when a student comes to class and transfers these conventions, learned in practical media exercises, to something s/he noticed on a television program and/or movie outside the classroom, and incorporates these into their media productions. I think this is because I enjoy watching them discover these concepts on their own as they operate the video equipment. I am impressed by how readily the students adopt and use technical skills and language of media production. I think the students were just as pleased with their newly acquired knowledge of media production, as illustrated in the following student comment:

> Before I started media production, I just questioned some of it, like why they did it or why they did it this way. And now, after taking the media course, I can understand. Like in movies, it can be an action or romance, whatever. Like how different shots can change the mood of things. Like a close up or long shot make it seem like different feelings. I practiced angle shots, you get to understand how it works and how they do that. Yeah, like I know how to do that, or I'd like to know how to do that.

Media production work seemed to interact with many of the students' more traditional literacy skills, strengthening each other reflexively. For some students, this meant increasing their efforts to advance their writing skills. Many began to be more conscious of different writing techniques. Working with the video cameras gave students different points of view, not only about the media and/or social issues, but also about ways of learning. Some realized that producing a video starts with a pen and consequently improved writing skills were necessary to produce better videos. Creating storyboards helped these students conceptualize their ideas, so that their writing was better organized and clearer. Knowing that there was an audience, besides a teacher, made writing a more purposeful activity. On many occasions, students sought my and/or their classmates advice on how best to word a sentence so that it was clearer, or how to be more economical with their words. Comments such as those below illustrate that not only did print become less of a threat for many ACE students, but also some of them realized that media technology and media production provided an avenue for expression of ideas:

> With the video cameras I've noticed that you can still get your skills done, but from a different perspective. Instead of worrying about spelling and punctuation you can do your work visually and vocally.

> I know that I'm the type of person who can't sit in a classroom and take notes. I can't just research from the book to paper, writing it down, putting it in my own words, typing it up and handing it in. It's not me. What I like doing is going out and researching it. Interviewing people. Finding out exactly what I want to find out.

Realising that there are different ways of learning also meant for some of the students that they actually could learn. The media projects enabled many of them to achieve success, and in turn developed their self-confidence and willingness to learn.

Growth and Improved Attitudes Toward Writing and Reading

Student comment:

> Well you understand what when you come back with your project you can say, hey I know this is what I learnt. I'm not just saying it, I'm showing it, I'm proving it to you. These are the people I interviewed, this is what I found out. It even shows how the project is made from beginning all the way to when its finished. And it's done not to the teacher's satisfaction. It's a good feeling handing in something like that. I did this, I'm proud of it. It also shows that somebody has the initiative to get off their butt. And why can't I?

The student's comment above illustrates that the media projects presented the students with real life, relevant problems. During the course of working on the media projects, they took many risks: an ironic twist for students considered 'at-risk'. Handling the technology, whether it was a video camera, the video editor, or a computer meant – for some students – taking a risk. Using technology engaged many of the ACE students so that they were less hesitant to engage in new skills, academic and interpersonal. They appeared to feel that the technology was less judgmental than a teacher might be, as expressed in the following student comment:

> I love using all kinds of technology. I love what is in the future, maybe that is why. When we work on the computers, the day goes by so fast.

Besides the technical skills the students were experiencing, the students developed self-confidence, something which few had ever experienced in the past. This is one of the most exciting aspects of observing them as they worked on the media projects. The students' improved self-confidence was evident in three areas:

1) Their approach and attitudes toward writing;
2) Working collaboratively with class mates; and
3) Dealing with the public.

Also there was an increasing willingness on the part of the students to take the risk of having someone else read their work. For already fragile egos, voluntarily asking for and then accepting criticism from a teacher and/or peers was, for many, an uneasy experience. In fact, the students willingly edited their work rather than having to be coerced into doing so. Rarely did any of them balk at being asked to edit the same work several times. They recognized the importance of rewrites and revision.

Why are the students willing to take such risks with their writing and actions, something most would not have done prior to working on the media projects? Part of the answer may have been in their awareness that there was an audience for their writing beyond a teacher. This realization made the activity more purposeful. A student wrote in her journal:

> I myself have found that by being exposed to the video camera and computers that my writing skills are more expressive and to the point. I really find that using these methods of computers, cameras and so on have been an enjoyable and educational experience. With these writing skills, I am sure that it will help me in the future, towards getting a good job.

I've changed as a writer since using the camera or computer because I write more than I used to. I used to write about seventy-five words, but now I write close to 200 words depending on the subject. I know that when I use a computer I write better. I don't know why, but I just do.

Many of the ACE students' attitudes towards reading also developed positively as illustrated below.

Me: Do you think doing the projects, using the cameras and other equipment, had any affect on your reading and writing skills?

H.J.: Doing the projects, I had to research so I had to read more. I write a bit faster. Now I take notes. t used to take me two days. Now I write more.

Me: Why do you think that is so?

H.J.: Well, it's because I know more about the subject. Like if some one had asked me about men in TV, I would have sat there and said "huh". Now I know more about the subject and ideas, ideas pop into my head, like movies we've watched which emphasise men and women in the workplace, and that helps me.

Collaboration

For many students, working in a group was a fairly new experience. Unfortunately, and ironically, at-risk students are not often given opportunities to work collaboratively. This is part of the stereotyped image of at-risk students, i.e. that they have difficulty working cooperatively.

Having the confidence to share what one has written and/or produced leads to shared and collaborative writing, and thus students are best able to develop their literate behavior of writing. Many ACE students realized the advantage that group work had in developing their literacy and their work. In the words of one student, working in a group was something I have had a lot of trouble adapting to. At the beginning of this year, many people adapted to this way of working faster than I did. The disadvantage was sharing ideas, and I'm still not used to that. I was taught to work on my own, with little teacher supervision. But the advantage of working in a group is that others will find your mistake 90% of the time, so no mistakes are made on the final draft of your work. You can also get better ideas by working with others. I remember one day a group member got a good idea and that did help our project.

There were times when the students experienced feelings of frustration and disappointment. The media projects required teamwork and organization, which resulted in some interesting lessons about what it means to work collaboratively and what it means to be a friend, noted in the following student remarks:

My view is that we had a bit of trouble following procedures correctly, but overall, our work was accomplished. Some of the troubles I found we had was that people who I was working with would not do the work and some of them didn't even go with us to the pool hall. I also found that I was doing my part plus the parts of my fellow workers so I was constantly working.

The student journal entries that follow illustrate W.L.'s perspective on how her group performed over a three-day period. The girl who wrote this series of journals conveyed a good grasp of how different members were feeling about the project, as well as about each other. She was also able to assess which students were actually pulling their weight. Furthermore, she suggested roles which best suited some of the group members.

I feel that the project is not moving along as fast as it could. Everyone seems to like the project. But if we do not work on it, it will not get done by itself. Tarra is often getting into arguments since Yohan is back. I think Kevin should be aloud working on the camera because he seems to like it and understand it even if he does not pass the test, some people are not good at tests.

Tomorrow Joey, Whip and Mat are going to the (television) station and they are painting the logo. Now Mat is working because it is fun. Jason is so tired of doing all the work, he thinks Mike should be helping more and concentrating on his part of the project. The people that have to work on the computers and cameras are the ones that are working and Jason the director is doing a very good job. Jason is always working non-stop. The boring part of working in a group is when your partner is not doing their share of the project.

Everyone is working so well. It is quiet without Mat. Jason is getting frustrated. Mike is not working much. Mike should forget the teachers and concentrate on helping Jason. Everyone did not take this project serious at the beginning so they are rushing at the end.

In describing her group members' performance, another student was willing to risk letting me know what my role should be as well:

The group has a lot of imagination. They work well but Yohan thinks to highly of himself and he has no right to boss the others. Mat, Eric, Joey and Whip do more individual work than group work but they are working well. Bruce understands his work, he is very well concentrated. Mr. Rother is always too busy and Patty is trying to finish her part but I think Mr. Rother should be concentrating on his part in the project instead of doing the director's job.

For others, collaboration was a totally worthwhile experience:

The positive thing that I found worked well was that we were well organized, we had everything planned out on what our roll's were. The work wasn't that hard of an assignment to complete because we all worked together equally. The project was fun to do and we got to investigate the arcade from a different perspective.

Excerpts from journals revealed a willingness by many ACE students to express opinions and feelings about daily events as well as the overall project progression. Many times in the course of a project, students went through a process of resisting a group member's ideas, negotiating, and then consenting to a collective agreement. For some students, offering solutions to problems was a form of risk-taking. The experience of participatory decision-making processes enabled many of them to learn conceptual, technical, and academic skills. But it also taught them a great deal about themselves through interactions with their classmates. Indeed, merely voicing their fears and concerns, both in their journals, to each other, and to me constituted risk taking.

The journal entries also reflect the persistence and self-discipline of some of the students who were determined to carry through with the projects. Some of them took the risk of volunteering for responsibilities that they were not always confident they could accomplish just so that the projects could be completed successfully. Contrary to what many educators believe, at-risk students, such as those in the ACE Program, really are interested in achieving academically and their own learning, and do not want to drop out.

The Literate Behavior of Public Expression

Earlier, I wrote that initially many of my students do not join in on class discussions and, metaphorically speaking, appear mute. They are afraid to take risks for fear of opening themselves up to criticism and/or ridicule, something many of them have unfortunately experienced often over the course of their school careers. Once they are well into the ACE Program, much of this reticence disappears. In fact, they not only develop the confidence to speak out among themselves, they also develop the confidence to express themselves to broader audiences. I think it is important to emphasise that at-risk students are rarely, if ever, given the opportunity to present to others what they have learned and/or what they already know in their school or in public forums. On a number of occasions, the ACE students participated in large public events outside of the classroom or their school, which required them to explain, discuss, and spontaneously respond to questions and/or debate issues. Following one of these events, an ACE student wrote in his journal:

I did learn quite a bit, and having to do a project on Gender helped me understand the importance of understanding the problems of Gender and Minorities in our society. I've become more aware so now I tell others. I also did like the presentation that I did.

The second opportunity for the students to be involved in was a public event including teachers and students from across Quebec. The topic was violence in the media. The ACE students were among many 'mainstream' high school students who risked sharing their personal beliefs and concerns.

Public occasions such as these gave the ACE students the opportunity to test out what they had learned about the media in the ACE Program. For example, a few of the students remarked that they thought it was "neat" to use and hear the media vocabulary related to analysis and production outside of the classroom setting, in a public forum.

Over the last several years, students in the ACE Program produced three telecasts aired on a community channel, each focusing on cooperative education programs. On each of such occasions, the ACE students were required to present their script, set design, and format ideas to the managing director of a community channel. The experience of being at the television studio and in the studio boardroom would have been overwhelming enough for many students. Having to provide arguments as well as express opinions and ideas about how the broadcast should develop only increased their uneasiness. Still, they managed to convey their plans in a professional and articulate manner. Similar examples occurred when guest speakers, who worked in the media industry, spoke or gave workshops to the class.

As I have indicated elsewhere, one of the dominant assumptions about at-risk students is that very often they have poor self-concepts. The examples above suggest otherwise, providing the students are given the opportunities to present themselves. I asked the students to discuss how they felt working on the media projects had helped them to develop their self-concepts:

The skills that helped to build my confidence was the phoning skills, because I'm not one to talk on the phone to much, and also I get nervous when I call someone, but since I did the media projects I don't get nervous on the phone anymore.

Another student wrote:

This year I sure did one thing, and that was learning how to beat my shyness which I think I did very well, it took lots of self confidence, something I had nothing of in the beginning of the year.

The major step to beating my lack of self confidence was going to work in another city. My shyness was beaten at work because I had to work with the public. We had to arrange meeting times with one of the people we interviewed, a doctor. It did takes us three weeks just to finish the interview with the doctor. It took a long time, but our project was successfully completed.

In the previous discussion, I presented examples of The Literate Behavior of Reading and The Literate Behavior of Writing.

In the first examples, I described the ACE students' Literate Behavior of Reading as they read/viewed two short films, *The Apprentice* and *The Oasis*, and a full length video, *Teenage Mutant Ninja Turtles*. The ACE students demonstrated several important characteristics of The Literate Behavior of Reading:

* Responding to texts affectively through their personal relationship to the text, and cognitively through their observations.

* Acknowledging, in writing and in print, that visual texts are sites for exploring one's position in society as autobiographies.

* Appropriating texts in order to rewrite it, making it their own.

* Predicting, analysing, interpreting and confirming their responses.

* Detecting and questioning the how and why of media's construction of reality, with special attention to ideological contexts through which texts are positioned.

* Performing several readings, each time learning and modifying their previous understandings.

* Identifying, linking and interpreting symbol and sign systems.

* Using oral and written language to articulate what they have learned about elements in media communications, including media language, genres and conventions.

* An understanding of denotation and connotation.

* An understanding of narrative structures.

* An awareness that reading is a meaning making process.

* Critical reading/viewing skills.

In the second examples, I described the ACE students' Literate Behavior of Writing in the course of producing two media projects, the first focusing on media industries – Marketing a Popular Culture Product – and the second, a socio-cultural research project: Gender and Minority Groups in Media, Society, and the Workplace. The students demonstrated an awareness of the following Literate Behaviors of Writing:

* The production and consumption of media texts.

* Intended messages aimed at a specific audience, its purpose, and forms of media messages.

* The economic basis of mass media production.

* The rhetoric of media language.

* The relationship between the form and content of media texts, recognising that each medium has its own grammar.

* Recognized the technical techniques used to produce media texts.

* Rehearsed, drafted, revised, edited and published/presented.

* Aesthetic aspects of media texts, so that they can evaluate their own likes and dislikes of media.

* That media contain ideological and value meanings in media texts.

* Formed bridges among the knowledge of media and media texts which they already possessed and extended that new knowledge into new areas of understanding.

As well as providing evidence of the Literate Behaviors listed above, I also conveyed another important aspect of Literate Behavior: that is, almost all of the ACE students were actively and continuously engaged.

In the next chapter, I elaborate on the significance of the previous discussion, specific to the ACE students, as well as provide a model of Literacy Education for at-risk students, and then suggest some questions for the future.

CHAPTER SIX
Reflections and Implications

Inclusion and Exclusion

Student comment:

> With the video cameras I've noticed that you can still get your skills done, but from a different perspective. Instead of worrying about spelling and punctuation you can do your work visually and vocally.

> I know that I'm the type of person who can't sit in a classroom and take notes. I can't just research from the book to paper, writing it down, putting it in my own words, typing it up and handing it in. It's not me. What I like doing is going out and researching it. Interviewing people. Finding out exactly what I want to find out.

> Well you understand when you come back with your project you can say, hey I know this is what I learnt. I'm not just saying it, I'm showing it, I am proving it to you. These are the people I interviewed, this is what I found out. It even shows how the project is made from beginning the project all the way to when its finished. And it's done not to the teacher's satisfaction. It's a good feeling handing in something like that. I did this, I'm proud of it. It also shows that somebody has the initiative to get off their butts. And why can't I?

Many of education's routines are founded in history as well as ideology. Since the Industrial Revolution, education has operated, with the best of stated intentions, on a system of inclusion and exclusion from mainstream schooling. For most at-risk students, fatigue and discouragement endured throughout the course of their elementary and high schooling – as they struggle with traditional educational practices – cause many not to continue. Stainback, Stainback, and Forest (1989) put forth the following argument:

If we want an integrated society in which all persons are considered of equal worth and as having equal rights, segregation in schools cannot be justified. That is, no defensible excuses or rationales can be offered, and no amount of scientific research can be conducted that will in the final analysis justify segregation. Segregation has no justification: it is simply unfair and morally wrong to segregate any students including those defined as disabled, from the mainstream of education (p. 4).

An educational system which segregates students, such as the ACE students, operates on what Freire (1973) referred to as "the banking system" (p. 52) where a teacher's role is to transmit knowledge to students by "depositing" information into students as they would deposit money into a bank. Taking this idea further, the currencies necessary for access to mainstream schooling, post-secondary education, and potentially "good jobs" include:

* A conformity to a traditional instructional system, which includes sitting in rows.

* Attending to teachers' presentations of material.

* Moving from classroom to classroom in set periods of time in which discrete subjects are taught.

* Formal testing, most of which is print-based.

* Traditional literacy skills in which students are given the information via the blackboard, overheads, etc.

* Reading teachers' handouts and/or from class textbooks.

* Listening to teacher talk and responding at length to their questions, but speaking very little.

* Generating print texts most of which are either highly restricted presentations, such as "objective" test genres or essays.

In fact, many students – such as the ones I teach – have actively resisted acquiring these currencies. Consequently, they have found themselves relegated to the fringes of education, with little possibility for upward mobility in schooling or vocationally.

We live in a society dominated by digital, multi-media information technology. Nevertheless, education is still predominately print-based for the most part. Most of the teaching that takes place in school is transmitted through print texts. Generally, visual and auditory texts are ignored, except when they are used as "audio-visual aids". In ignoring the use and study of these texts in their own right, teachers are ignoring other forms of literacy, and what it means to be really literate in a multi-media society. Postman (1971) echoes my thoughts:

> The term universal literacy simply meant the hope that all men [sic] could have made available to them reading and writing. But the term continues to change as the means of communication change. Today literacy is the skill with which man manipulates the many media of mass communication. Reading and writing are still important. But much more is required in a multi-media age (pp. 26 27).

The ACE Students' Struggle for Literacy

As a result of my experiences with the ACE Students, I have come to the conclusion that they are literate and that traditional practices of literacy education such as those I have described above have prevented us as teachers from acknowledging their literacy. Schooling's notion of literacy which uses de-contextualized print texts as the only data source to determine students' literacy reflects almost exactly Street's (1984) characterization of a model of literacy that is outdated and inadequate. The principal assumption of the "autonomous model" is that literacy is largely determined by performance on "essay texts", and from that performance accessors generalize broadly from what is, in fact, a narrow culture-specific practice. Other features of the model include the following assumptions:

* There is a single direction in which literacy development can be traced, and are all the direct result of that development: 'progress', 'civilization', individual liberty and social mobility.

* That literacy is distinguishable from schooling.

* That literacy can be isolated as an independent variable and the consequent claim that we can study its consequences.

* That the consequences are represented in terms of cognitive skills and/or economic 'take off'. (p. 2).

Adherence to this above notion of literacy has had disastrous consequences for the kinds of students who are "at-risk". In spite of the fact that I have discovered how literate my ACE students are in reading and writing their texts, I continue to be frustrated by the refusal of many current school system to relinquish its hold on this "autonomous model" and the concomitant consequences that result. For the ACE students, their "illiteracy" will continue to result in a:

> struggle for development, justice, greater equality, respect of cultures and recognition of human dignity of all and the claims of each to an economic, social and political stake in society and the fruits which derive therefrom (UNESCO, 1989, p. 4).

Over the last thirty years, many educators have tried to boost the self-esteem of at-risk students through various "feel good" approaches and activities, but these educators have not fundamentally changed their conceptualisations of literacy or pedagogy.

Traditional methods and approaches have inadvertently contributed to poor feelings of self-worth and a lack of interest in school. The kind of Media Education Curriculum that I have used with the ACE Students challenged, involved, and encouraged the these at-risk students to develop their overall literacy. Several of the students have said that it was one of the principal reasons for their staying in school.

J.A. was one of my students who, on her own, decided that the "regular program" was not meeting her needs and conversely she was not able to meet its demands, and decided that the ACE Program might help. In her journal, she wrote:

> I was one of those students who felt I was at a dead end. I thought there was no help for me and everyone, including myself, thought I was a lost cause. I started to have very low self-esteem.

> After a couple of weeks in the ACE Program, my self-esteem soared. I started feeling good about myself. I finally felt I had a place in school. I started getting active and happy in doing my assigned tasks. I went to school everyday with a smile rather than a frown. It felt good waking up in the morning.

On the basis of my experience with the ACE students, I wish to argue that education needs to rethink how it approaches literacy so that it recognizes:

1. Reading and writing as socio-cultural practices that are context bound.
2. That texts students are asked to read and write include both print and audio-visual forms.
3. That texts students are asked to read have relevancy to them (i.e., that they take cognizance of the students' own socio-cultural contexts) and that students' response to these texts form the basis of their literacy education. One of the ways that would ensure the authenticity and relevancy of responses is to have students choose texts.
4. That the data sources used to assess students' literacy take cognizance of and reflect the context-bound nature of literacy practices of these young people.

I have attempted throughout to situate literacy within a broader set of individual and social competencies. I have chosen to focus on ways in which the ACE students exhibited their own form of literate behaviors in the process of reading and writing media texts. I believe that the Media Education Curriculum I developed enabled me to identify some of the parameters of the ACE students' literacy and to confirm the effectiveness of the Media Education Curriculum and the pedagogy that I used in developing the literate abilities of the ACE students.

A Broader Picture of Literate Behavior

My observations of the ACE students' literate behaviors echo many of the concepts provided by English Language Arts and Media Education theorists, which I discussed earlier.

The ACE students read – they understood and responded to written and visual languages. They wrote – they used print, oral/aural, and visual forms of language within a social context for specific and relevant purposes and for different audiences. Britton (1975) refers to these activities of reading and writing means of coming to terms with ideas and experiences and of communicating with others. That is, the expressive, transactional and poetic functions of language.

In the process of reading and dialoguing about the video texts, the students became aware of how the texts related to their own status and experiences. Once they were able to make personal meaning from the texts, they were then able to articulate that meaning to the rest of the class. This is what Moffet and Wagner (1976) suggested about reading and writing involving the ability to move from interior dialog based on personal values and experiences to social speech. Rosenblatt's (1978) notion of reading as a transactional process in which readers act upon texts by reconstructing them, explains the ACE students' ability to make connections between their life experiences and the various ideas and experiences represented in *The Apprentice* and *The Oasis*. The students' retelling of these texts, based on their own life experiences, is Willinsky's (1991) second principle of postmodern literacy, which argues that texts are not fixed creations, but develop through collaboration and appropriation of texts that already exist. In their analysis of situation comedies, the ACE students participated first as readers and then as writers and critics, Willinsky's third principle of postmodern literacy. The students were highly critical of these television programs based on their own life experiences, as well as their experiences with media texts.

Further, the students reading of the cultural signs in the *Teenage Mutant Ninja Turtles* are examples of McCormick, Waller, and Flower's (1992) notion of polyvalent reading, in which individual readers construct meaning according to their literary and ideological repertoires. Many of the students had fairly sophisticated understandings of the dimensions of representation, and detected biases, stereotypes, omissions and inconsistencies in the Ninja Turtles.

In the process of working on the Marketing Project, many of the ACE students described the links between the production and ownership of popular culture texts. For example, each group gave itself a company name and an associated trademark and slogan. I recall one student forcefully stating that "his company" needed to place a copyright symbol on their package so that other groups of students would not be able to steal their ideas. This led to each group doing the same. Another instance that illustrates the students' knowledge of ownership occurred during the phone call M.D. and his group made to the record store company regarding their *Musical Carpet.* After the phone call, M.D. worried that his groups' idea might be "stolen" by the record company. Thus, as Willinsky (1991) suggests, they appreciated that the postmodern world is a mixed economy of art and commerce, encompassing popular cultural forms.

In addition, I found links of the ACE students' literate behaviors to many of the English Language Arts educators/theorists. The impact of the kind of Media Education Curriculum I used enabled the ACE students to:

* Develop a sophisticated understanding of and critical stance toward the dominant means of communication in their lives: the mass media.

* Build their language skills so that they are able to conceptualise ideas for themselves and others.

* Express those ideas in words, images and sounds.

* Encode those ideas in organized, sequential, and clear presentations, which includes an articulation of their personal sensibilities.

* Participate openly in an exchange of ideas and opinions
  as scholars/producers of media texts.

* Use inquiry and critical thinking skills to develop
  their interests.

* Develop self expression and feeling of self worth.

The ACE students, like most other students, bring the consumption of thousands of hours of viewing, listening and interacting with media to school, and have informally acquired many of the literate behaviors I described, that is, The Literate Behavior of Reading and Writing. In other words, students, such as those in the ACE Program, come to school with an already developed repertoire of literate behaviors that need to be fully acknowledged, organized, and exploited within the context of schooling.

Curriculum

In the Media Education Curriculum I designed, I included elements of the conceptual framework: texts, audience and production developed by Dick (1990). The students critically analyzed media texts, such as *The Apprentice, The Oasis* and *Teenage Mutant Ninja Turtles*, as well as situation comedies. They also constructed media texts, such as the television, radio, and print advertisements for the Marketing projects.

Generally, media-oriented curricula developed for at-risk students have focused on the use of technology rather than on the development of literacy. There is a strong emphasis on equipment manipulation and production, and little on practical reflection. The thinking is that these students do not possess higher level thinking ability necessary to deal with analytical work. I think the examples, taken from ACE student journals, which follow dispel this notion.

During a discussion of minority groups, it became obvious that K.H. had very strong and biased opinions regarding the media's image of black and white people. While she claimed not to be "prejudiced", she felt that media's image was biased in favor of blacks. She interpreted a rap song she heard outside of school this way:

In the media some rap songs create a terrible image of Caucasians. The lyrics mention how difficult black peoples lives are living in dangerous communities and being victims. White people are portrayed in their rich homes in safe towns not giving any thought to reckless violence.

S.C.'s opinion regarding the image of women in the media was just as obvious as K.H.'s views about media's image of blacks and whites. S.C. contrasted two situation comedies she viewed at home:

One program that really shows sexism is *Home Improvement*. Tim is always putting women down, and he never allows Jill, his wife, to use his tools. Tim's always mentioning that a women's place is in the kitchen. A show that proves the opposite is *Grace Under Fire*, which illustrates how women can survive without a man around the house. She even works in a non-traditional job.

These excerpts also demonstrate what Smith (1988) said about how children learn reading, writing and literacy outside of school. Most of the ACE students have implicit understanding and critical awareness of popular media texts. The media curriculum used in the ACE Program helped them to reflect, articulate, and expand upon what they knew about the media they consumed. In doing so, I believe the students began to see themselves as readers and writers who deserved to be "members" in what Smith called "the literacy club". They also exhibited the following eligibility requirements for entry into the club:

1. Their reading of the media texts was meaningful and purposeful to them personally.

2. They related and added what they read in the texts to their personal repertoires.

3. They were continuously active during the media projects.

4. They were able to relate the learning they acquired in the media projects to their everyday lives.

5. They collaborated both in the reading of the media texts and the media projects.

The Teaching Approach:
A Retrospective Look at the Pedagogy

Here I reflect back to the kind of environment that I provided, which enabled me to identify the ACE students' literate behavior. I want to describe the teaching approaches I used in the ACE Program, because I firmly believe that they enabled me to tease out the students' literate behaviors.

The Media Education Curriculum I designed provided the ACE students with non-threatening, non-competitive experiences, rich in reading (viewing) and writing (producing). It featured projects through which the students could dialog, reflect, access, and evaluate ideas and information. In following this curriculum, the ACE students developed a more meaningful understanding of themselves and the concepts at the heart of English Language Arts and Media Education.

Building on work by educators and theorists such as Dewey, Vygotsky, and Freire, I employed a constructivist, project-based approach, and student-centered pedagogy. I attempted to ensure that the students were actively involved in contextualised, real world problems. I made sure that the ACE classroom was a living entity that invited concrete, inductive, and spirited learning. I exploited the students' mindset, which tended to operate in the present tense, and was geared to active participation.

Teaching Practice

As I explained elsewhere, the ACE students were more comfortable working in extended blocks of time instead of in fifty-minute periods, each devoted to a separate subject. However, it was necessary for me to ensure that I was covering all of the subjects in the ACE Program: English, Math, French, Life Skills, and World of Work. Consequently, I designed The ACE Program as an interdisciplinary curriculum. Class time is not divided into discrete periods. As the ACE Students were with me the whole day over a two-year period, I did not have to worry about taking time away from another subject, or another teacher; students were free to work on one specific aspect of their project for extended periods of time. Students could also venture outside of the school into the local community to do research or interview various people for their project without having to worry about being back in time for another class.

Negotiating Curriculum

The curriculum was thematically-based, and was actually negotiated with the students. So the Gender and Minority Groups in the Media and Society theme originally came from units on family and getting along with people. Following is a description of how I conducted classes on the Gender and Minority Group theme. It is typical of my overall teaching approach.

After writing the title of the theme on the overhead, I asked the students to speculate what the theme might be about. My intent was to get some ideas about the direction they might want to take. This was followed by asking them to provide me with titles of books, television programs, movies, magazines, games, and so on, that dealt in some way with the topic we were working on at a specific time, such as media's image of men and women in the workplace. I have always considered my students my first resource.

Using a list of texts, the students and I chose one for a close reading, usually a television program and/or movie, which over the next day or two we "read" and analyzed. I subsequently scrounged print-based texts, such as short stories, poems, and magazine articles, which we could also use for our initial discussions. The students were also required to choose a book from the library, or from home. One class per day was devoted to just reading. Many ACE students who had never completed an entire book before did so when given this class time.

A Dialogic Approach to Analyzing Texts

The approach I took analysing the texts with the students is best characterised by Freire (1973) as a dialog which involves an "I-Thou relationship between two subjects" (p. 52) in which the students and I engaged in a two-way communication. Masterman (1985) characterizes dialog as a "genuine sharing of power" (p. 33) in which each participant listens carefully and responds to what has been said. The intent is to come to a better understanding of the issue or topic at hand.

Generally speaking, I adopted the following approach to working with texts. I began by asking the students their general responses to the text. For example, I asked, "Did you like it? Why? What was it about?" Then, in small groups, the students would talk in greater detail about their response to the text, and any observations made about it. A recorder took notes. We would then hold a class dialog of what our responses to the text were and what we learned about it. At that time, we would also review segments of the text, usually a number of times, in order to confirm our responses and observations. Following our public discussion, the students individually wrote their responses in their notebooks. The responses were subsequently used as springboards for finally writing about the texts, or for their projects. I collected the notebooks either the same day or allowed them to complete the responses and submit them the next day.

The Issue of Power

The next few days were spent dialoguing openly about the texts we read. Recall the amount of talking and thinking out loud that took place as we read *The Apprentice*, *The Oasis*, and *Teenage Mutant Ninja Turtles*. As in the case of *The Apprentice*, I did not have as strong an interpretation of the text as some of the students did. Many of the students took pleasure when they realized that I did not understand *The Apprentice* to the same depth that they did. They enjoyed watching me grope, struggling to compose my own understanding of the text. This reminds me of Freire's (1970) comment that, "through dialog the teacher of the student ceases to exist and a new term emerges; the teacher with the students" (p. 67). According to Freire, knowledge does not only belong to the teacher, but also to the students. By revealing that I was not the all-knower, the students felt that they had something to bring to the learning, to offer to their classmates and me. In such instances, neither I nor they occupied a special position in the class hierarchy. Masterman (1985) calls this non-hierarchical teaching which promotes reflection, critical thinking within a group-focused, action-oriented atmosphere. Barnes (1992) refers to this type of teaching as interpretive.

I should make it clear that the non hierarchical teaching approach that

I describe here does not imply that I relinquished teacher control. While a dialogical and non-hierarchical approach does involve a sharing of power, a differential power relationship continues to exist with me in control. Indeed, the type of teaching approach here can be risky, since students might consider that a teacher's willingness to dialog about, rather than transmit, ideas (Barnes, 1992) suggests that s/he wishes to become one of the group.

While I had knowledge of the formal processes and concepts of English Language Arts and Media Education, the students also had expertise in some of the processes; much of the content of the texts we examined together, and especially in making connections among the texts and their own real life experiences. You may recall the richness of the ACE students' responses to *The Apprentice* and *The Oasis* as we discussed the words, images, and sounds that enabled them to make links to their own lives. This dimension of my teaching approach focuses on personal response, which requires the students to think about what elements of their own repertoires they can bring to a text, and to the classroom.

Interdependancy, Independance, and Inclusiveness

There are several things I want to say about the reading experiences that I think contributed to generating evidence of the ACE students' literate behavior. One concerns twin notions of interdependency and independence, the other issue is inclusiveness.

In the ACE Program, the students and I nurtured each other's ideas, constructing our own interpretations of the texts. As we talked about the videos, I acted as secretary, writing the students' ideas on the blackboard so that we could all see each other's contributions to the discussion, and the results of our individual and collective thinking. This approach enabled the students to:

1. Understand that not everyone reads stories the same way.

2. That each can read the same text differently.

3. That each has the ability to add to the shared meaning.

By using the responses of their fellow classmates' writing on the board, the students were able to tease out ideas, gradually progressing to more sophisticated understandings of the texts. I am reminded here of what Dewey (1934) wrote how education comes about through the inspiration a student gets from those with whom he interacts, including his/her classmates and his/her teacher. The technique of open dialog of student responses and writing them on the board also gave the students opportunities to voice uncertainties about ideas. They realized that not knowing and/or questioning their own ideas was acceptable, and did not mean that they were "stupid".

It occurred to me that some of the ACE students who do not usually have the confidence of many of their classmates – and, in fact, are considered outcasts by some – aren't afraid to speak up when we discuss media texts. They ask questions and offer response, seemingly without concern of ridicule. And they aren't ridiculed. E.V. and P.T. are examples. Often, the feedback given to students helped them clarify their ideas. Freire (1970) wrote: "education is a live and creative dialog in which everyone knows something and does not know others, in which we all seek together to know more" (p. 113).

A second, and what I consider an extremely important aspect of the socialization experiences described above, is the issue of inclusiveness. Approaching the reading experiences through dialog and discussion created an inclusive reading environment. Grade and/or credit levels, and social status in the class, were inconsequential. The reading experiences that occurred let each student see that his/her idea had value and contributed to our collective understanding, something which was especially important for the traditionally weaker students. Frequently, we discourage weaker students from participating by trying to draw out more than what they are able to offer "on the spot". By prodding too much, many of these students are reluctant to take risks, and tend to draw away from these situations. In creating an inclusive atmosphere, all of the students were encouraged to continue reading and to actively participate.

Developing the ACE Students' Research Projects

After having spent several days, dialoguing, reading, viewing, and writing, I asked the students, in groups, to compose a thesis statement about a specific theme in the text that we had been reading which they would like to prove or disprove, or a question they would like to investigate.

Their ideas for inquiry were then placed onto the overhead. Each group brainstormed ways that they might go about their inquiry. The only requirements I placed here were that they had to use print, non-print, and/or audio visual sources. The other requirement was that their final submission included a written, oral, and audio-visual presentation. The students' ideas included such inquiry techniques as surveys and interviews. My role here was to help them develop the survey questionnaires and prepare for the interviews. I also coached them, pointing them toward suitable resources. In most instances, the students did the actual locating of information or contacting various individuals to interview. Locating human resources for information involved the students in authentic communication activities, such as calling on the telephone, writing, and faxing business letters, e-mailing and so on. Over the next few weeks, the students worked on their projects.

The Use of Time

The duration of some of the projects is an interesting issue. I did not have formal daily lesson plans. To be frank, I found early in my career that lesson plans were stifling and constraining. In fact, I only had an approximation of the amount of time the projects would last. This was not based so much on the students' ability as it was the level of their engagement. Since I had the luxury of working with the students all day and was not bound to an inflexible schedule, I let the projects continue as long as the students displayed interest. Remember that some of the students reacted angrily when I attempted to put closure to reading *The Apprentice* as well as when I threatened to reinstate the fifty minute class period. They told me in their own way that they had to have some say in how and in what time frame they developed knowledge. Frankly, in most instances, it was not my intention that the projects lasted such an extended period of time, but the projects took on lives of their own, and the students gave life to the projects. The only time constraint was that each project did not last more than one term. Noteworthy, is the students' engagement, considering that at-risk students lose interest in most school assignments quickly (this should not be confused with the notion of short attention spans). Dewey (1934) considered interest an indication of 'growing power and dawning capacities'. According to Dewey, the role of the teachers is to identify and encourage such power.

In most instances, the final stage of the projects was the submission of a written, audio-visual and oral presentation to the class. In many cases, we celebrated the end of a theme with a broad, informal discussion of the overall project and/or a "showing off" of the projects to invited guests such as the school's and or school board's administration.

The approaches I have described above were experience-based. They were also oriented toward active, concrete, inductive and kinesthetic learning. The students were actively involved in reading, talking, writing, viewing, or producing. The atmosphere was alive. In most instances, the students were stimulated. I trusted the students to learn, and they trusted me to get out of their way and let them learn. I encouraged the students to develop their own patterns of addressing the problems they were pursuing. I let them organize their learning strategies, and they let me in on their learning as a mentor and coach. There was no set routine to the learning. While I had an idea of the direction I wanted the class to go in, the initial reading/viewing activities, the students shaped and implemented the days which followed. Some days they worked in class, on others, with the required preparations, their investigations took them outside of the class into the larger community. Some days they worked in the classroom at their desks, on others they were scattered about on computers, video editing, or hidden in a closet producing a radio show. Vygotsky (1978) might have referred to this approach as 'taking advantage of the zone of proximal development', in which a student is guided to solve problems on his own, using all of his/her prior understanding (scientific conceptual knowledge). It was messy learning, but it was real learning. It was the kind of learning that created a sense of community.

CHAPTER SEVEN
A Literacy Curriculum Model
for At-Risk High School Students

I began this discussion with an exploration of the theoretical concepts of English Language Arts and Media Education that would provide a framework for investigating the ACE students' literate behaviors of reading and writing. I explored links among the concepts and theories of English Language Arts Curriculum, and the Media Education Curriculum I designed in the ACE Program, and their relationship to the literate behaviors displayed by the ACE students themselves in different contexts.

Buckingham argues that there is a paradoxical relationship among English and Media Education. In his article, *English and Media Studies: Making the Difference*, (1993b) he points out the conceptual and practical differences between the two disciplines. While I acknowledge that these differences exist for some English and Media Education theorists, I prefer to believe in fundamental intertwined relationships among English Language Arts and Media Education theory, curriculum, and pedagogy. These relationships can be expressed in terms of how we understand literacy in schools: more precisely, in terms of literate behaviors.

Through the 1970s, 80s, and early 90s there has been a shift in the conceptualization of English Language Education. English educators have become Language Arts educators who recognize that as language develops, it serves important human functions – expressive, transactional and poetic (e.g., Britton, 1975) – is organized into forms of oral, written, and visual discourse (e.g., Moffett & Wagner, 1976), is developed in social contexts (e.g., Bruffee, 1986), serves intentions of writers (Graves, 1983) and readers (Rosenblatt, 1978), and is generated for audiences (Doughty, Pearce and Thornton, 1976).

English Language Arts education is about providing learners with opportunities to use and investigate language in all its various dimensions, so that they can come to terms with the ideas of the world in which they live and can act critically, creatively, and consciously on that world (see for example, Greene, 1988). Reading and writing are seen as complex processes that have cognitive, social, and cultural dimensions. For English Language Arts educators, reading includes all kinds of text: from Shakespeare to shopping malls, from *Sesame Street* to the *Wall Street Journal*; writing means producing a television commercial, performing a radio talk show, or writing an essay on the computer. To be sure, much of the above conceptualization has been influenced by developments in other fields, such as Communications and Linguistics. However, I would argue that within the field of English education, the preconditions existed for the ready adoption of these ideas, and that many aspects have preceded developments in both the fields of Communication and Media Education.

It is significant that many of the major theoreticians/practitioners in the field of Media Education either come from or write from the English education community: Len Masterman, David Buckingham, Andrew Hart (Britain); Robyn Quin and Barrie McMahon (Australia); Barry Duncan, Neil Anderson, Donna Carpenter, Jack Livesley, Chris Worsnop, and Rick Shepherd (Canada.)

A Changing Conceptualization of Literacy

These changes in view have resulted in a changing conceptualization of Literacy. We have moved beyond earlier considerations involving the functional aspects of language, such as ordinary everyday communication or being able to understand and express oneself in the workplace. In describing the new Literacy, John Willinsky (1991) establishes some prime considerations that have developed from English Language Arts theory and practice:

* What counts is the use of language rather than the medium or technology.

* Texts are not fixed creations, but develop through collaboration and appropriation of texts that already exist.

* All texts, oral, written and visual are dependent on the socio-cultural meaning of signs.

* Postmodern literacy acknowledges the contribution of mainstream popular culture forms as sites for exploring the relationship between one's position in society and the socio-political ideologies in society.

* Postmodern literacy endorses the theoretical and production aspects of Media Studies in order to help students demystify media texts.

* Postmodern literacy is critical literacy that, through the use of language, promotes public consciousness of social, cultural, and economic ideologies.

In the introduction to *Media Files*, Emery et al. (1995), an attempt was made to consolidate for English teachers in Quebec, the evolution of English Language Arts theory and Willinsky's notion of postmodern literacy. First, we teachers are encouraged to reconceive texts as cultural artifacts: a weaving together of signs – drawn from an individual's experiences with them as a member of a culture – created for the purpose of communicating ideas.

Texts, therefore, include not only print (fiction and non-fiction), but radio, television and film, environments such as shopping malls, and toys like Barbie and GI Joe dolls. (We have used the word "signs": a term for objects, icons, symbols and/or words, comprising a signifier and a signified – instead of "words" or "symbols", because the term more accurately applies to all forms of language, including diversified media, as well as traditional forms of language.) (Emery et al., 1995, p. 5).

Next, the terms repertoire (developed from McCormick, Waller and Flower, 1992) and ideology are introduced:

This [repertoire] refers to a combination of knowledge, experiences, habits, norms conventions and assumptions that are brought to bear by an individual in any specific reading or writing instance . . . For purposes of our discussion [of Literacy], we conceive of two aspects or categories of repertoire: that which includes matters related to discourse and its forms – medium, genre, mode rhetoric and code; and that which includes matters of ideology. Both aspects of repertoire are shaped by social, cultural, historical and gendered experiences (Emery et al., 1995, p. 5).

Reading, as suggested in the *Media Files*, is a transactional process in which a reader and her/his repertoire meet a text and its author's or producer's repertoire(s). Reading is a cognitive act in which readers, because they attach different meanings to the signs of a text, help to create the texts they read. Thus, different readers may make sense of the same text in quite different ways. To some extent, the diversity of readings may be invited or allowed by the nature of the text itself. Furthermore, because readers may read a range of different texts (i.e., have different repertoires), this will affect the reading of a particular text. Reading is, at the

MEDIA EDUCATION	ENGLISH LANGUAGE ARTS
Literate Behaviour of Reading	**Literate Behavious of Writing**
Response Critique · Understand	**Response** Aesthetic · Efferent
Analysis Purpose · Industry · Media · language / genre · Audience	**Analysis** Purpose · Context · Language · form / genre · Audience
Literate Behaviour of Writing Use of language forms · Audio · Visual · Print	**Literate Behaviour of Writing** Use of language forms · Audio · Visual · Print
Key Concepts Construct reality · Industry / production · Aesthetic	**Functions of Language** Expressive · Transactional · Progressive
Processes Plan · Organize · Revise · Edit · Present	**Processes** Rehearse · Draft · Revise · Edit · Publish
Curricular Approaches Collaborative · Project-Based · Process-oriented	**Curricular Approach** Collaborate · Project-Based · Process-oriented
Pedagogical Approaches Non-Hierarchical	**Pedagogical Approaches** Interpretive / Negotiated

Figure 8

same time, a social process in that the meaning of a text is not established by a reader in isolation, but rather, through social interaction and principally through talk. How individuals talk about and use what they read both shape and reflect their own cultural identities. Readers also develop hypotheses about how other people read and form alliances with other individuals who read like they do. They also define themselves socially and culturally in terms of tastes and preferences, in terms of what they are not as well as what they are (see Buckingham and Sefton Green, 1994). In short, in any given encounter with a text, an immensely complex interplay of repertoires takes place. Writing is also a process that involves writers using complex discursive and general repertoires to construct texts for real or imagined readers/audiences, who "read" them. Like reading, writing is a complex cognitive activity in which individuals construct texts for others using media modes and codes of communication, according to forms and conventions characteristic of discourse in specific contexts. It too is simultaneously a social process in that writers construct discourse from certain socio-cultural communities or contexts to others within or outside these communities or contexts, bringing to bear complex rhetorical strategies that enable them to articulate who they are as much as what they have to say. Furthermore, reading and writing are not seen as discrete activities, but as simultaneously interactive processes so that even when readers act "in the reading mode" they are constructing (i.e., writing) meaning; when writers write they read the meanings of what they write not only as readers of themselves but also acting in the capacity of imagined other readers of their texts.

Therefore, within the framework of the above understandings, literacy constitutes the individual's conscious use of new or expanding repertoires as a reader and a writer. Literate behavior is the ensemble of processes individuals – usually in social groupings or discourse communities – undertake in developing that consciousness.

As I have stated elsewhere, my focus has been on how Media Education Curriculum might be considered a site for at-risk students' struggle for literacy. The connections I have made between English Language Arts and Media Education are gathered as the ACE students read the video texts and wrote their media projects.

Figure 8, on the previous page, shows the relationship among English Language Arts Education, Media Education, and Literate Behaviors of

Reading and Writing. The model presents a broad view of the position of English Language Arts and Media Education within the context of literacy. It illustrates that conceptualizations of literacy arise out of socio-cultural contexts (Street, 1984). The elements are constantly interacting in the actual events of teaching and learning. Think of this as a three-dimensional model in which none of the elements are in any particular hierarchical order.

The Literate Behavior of Reading

Response

I am using the phrase "responding to" in the same way that Rosenblatt (1968) talked about the transactional process in which readers reconstruct meaning in texts, and McCormick, Waller and Flower's (1992) notion of reading as an active process. From a Media Education point of view, I see "responding to" similar to Masterman's (1990) key concept of Media Education, which states that audiences negotiate meaning. In this instance, I am thinking of audience as single readers, albeit acting as members of social groups of readers.

The ACE students responded to the video texts in much the same way that all readers respond to print texts They read the texts looking to understand the plot, (efferently), and at the same time, based on their personal positions and experiences, as critics, (aesthetically). Reading both traditional and media texts is a transactional process in which a reader and his/her repertoire meets a text and its repertoire. This supports the reading dimension of literacy as described it in the Media Files (Emery et al., 1995).

Analysis

How a reader approaches a print and/or media text, and subsequently responds to it, depends on knowledge of language/media forms and genres, the audience at which it is aimed, its specific purpose, and the context in which it is read (Doughty, Pearce, & Thornton, 1976; Masterman, 1985). One of the contexts in which a media text must be considered is the context of "industry". Buckingham and Sefton-Green

(1994) note that Media Education teachers deal with the issue of industry in the production, ownership, and selling of media texts, while English teachers do not. However, given English Language Arts' conceptual understanding of context, purpose, and audience, there is no theoretical reason why English teachers cannot incorporate "industry".

The Literate Behavior of Writing

Understanding language forms and genres also means understanding that form and content are closely related as well, and that each medium has its own grammar and codifies reality in unique ways (see "Key Concepts" in Association for Media Literacy's *Media Literacy Resource Guide*, 1989, p. 10). *Figure 8* illustrates the relationship among the various forms of language in English Language Arts – aural, visual, print, and Media Education – audio, visual, and print.

There were several instances when ACE students exhibited their understanding of the conventions used in various media texts, and the links between language form and content. Examples of these understandings include their discussions about advertisements and situation comedies, and how their genres, audiences, purposes, and contexts could be identified by: the specific spoken language – vocabulary, dialect; sound effects and music; and/or the specific production techniques – camera shots, angles, movement, pacing. Their media projects displayed their understanding of how language forms and media languages could be manipulated for specific audiences, purposes and contexts.

The Key Concepts/Functions of Language

According to Britton's "transactional function" of language, we attempt to advise, persuade, or inform. This is precisely what occurs in most mass media texts, especially when one considers the industry dimension.

Simultaneously, we attempt to aesthetically please both the author and the reader (see *Media Literacy Resource Guide*, 1989, Key Concept 8), attending to the poetic function (Britton, 1975).

Throughout the writing process, whether we are writing a report, an advertisement or a documentary, we use an "expressive" function of language in order to construct our own sense of reality for our readers. In producing mini-documentaries in the Gender and Minority projects, and print and non print advertisements in their Marketing Projects, ACE students used transactional, poetic, and expressive forms of writing.

Processes

Writing and/or producing both a print and a media text invoke similar processes: rehearsing/planning, drafting/organizing, revising, editing and publishing/presenting. Both writing and media productions begin with imagining the message that is to be conveyed to an audience and the words/images which will create the intended message. All kinds of texts involve the printed word at some stage of their development.

So for instance, before embarking on their media productions, the ACE students first met in groups and rehearsed what message they wanted to create in their productions, and planned how they were going to go about creating the message. The students then drafted a production proposal and organized themselves according to the people, places, and things which they needed to complete their productions. Part of the organization also included revising, drafting and editing the production.

Curricular/ Pedagogical Approaches

I have found that the curricular approaches that feature collaboration, are project-based, and focus on processes and the development of capabilities lend themselves well to both Media Education and English Language Arts Education. Furthermore, I see great similarity in the pedagogical approaches advocated by Masterman (Media Education), Barnes, and Boomer (English Language Arts Education): non-hierarchical; interpretative and negotiated.

I now see my English Language Arts and Media Education Curriculum as Literacy Education for at-risk students. I strongly believe that this notion of Literacy Education has value for other teachers and students in alternative programs, who are struggling with conventional teaching and learning practices.

Some Questions for the Future

It seems only fitting that the words used to set the scene for possible future research come from something a student found in a local newspaper, which she passed on to me. L.G. wrote:

> I fully realize that you have not succeeded in answering all of my questions. In fact, I feel that you have not answered any of them completely. But the answers I have found only serve to raise a whole set of new questions, which only lead to more questions, some of which I didn't even realize were questions. In some ways, I feel that I am as confused as ever, but on a higher level, and about more important things.

When I asked L.G why she wrote this for me, she explained that the way I taught her was not the kind of teaching she was used to; the kind that always seemed to end with answers, most often someone else's. She went on to explain that what I did was to encourage and give her the confidence to ask more questions from the answers she already had or those she discovered in the course of exploring some of the topics we covered in the ACE Program. I like to think that her comments above were a kind of thank you.

And like L.G, I find solace in knowing that I too am confused on a higher level, and about increasingly important things. Some of the questions which have arisen as a result of the experiences described in this book, and which are points for future qualitative explorations are:

1. To what extent are the observations I made about the responses of the ACE students to my Media Education Curriculum idiosyncratic? More studies of Media Education Curriculum and Pedagogy with at-risk students should be undertaken.

2. I presented indications that the ACE students were able to translate their literate interpretations and constructions of media texts into more traditional forms, but much more investigative work needs to be done on this, both with at-risk and mainstream students.

3. Perhaps the most important questions are the curricular and pedagogical ones. One question is, "to what extent are we willing to rethink who, how, and what we are teaching in order to develop approaches that motivate and encourage, not only students who are struggling with conventional schooling practices, but also all students?" A broader question is implicated: "what types of investigations must educators perform regarding factors which lead schooling to resist the kind of model I presented earlier, and what changes in education must occur if such a model is to work?"

REFERENCES

Alvarado, M. (1977). L'initiation aux medias en Europe occidentale: le Royaume Uni. In UNESCO (Ed.), *Etude des medias dans l'enseignement* (pp 42-53). Etudes et documents d'information, no. 80, Paris: UNESCO.

Alvarado, M., & Boyd Barrett, O. (Eds.). (1992). *Media education: An introduction.* London: British Film Institute in partnership with The Open University.

Alvarado, M., & Ferguson, B. (1983). The curriculum, media studies and discurvity, *Screen, 24*(3), 20-34.

Alvarado, M., Gutch, R., & Wollen, T. (1987). *Learning the media: An introduction to media teaching.* London: Macmillan.

Anderson, G., Herr, K., & Nihlen, S. (1994). *Studying your own school: An educator's guide to qualitative practitioner research.* Thousand Oaks, Calif.: Corwin Press.

Anderson, J. A., & Meyer, T. (1988). *Mediated communication: A social action perspective.* Newbury Park: Sage.

Applebee, A. N. (1974). *Tradition and reform in the teaching of English.* Urbana, Ill: National Council of Teachers of English.

Applebee, A. N. (1977). *A survey of teaching conditions in English.* Urbana, Ill: National Council of Teachers of English.

Association for Media Literacy. (1989). *Media literacy resource guide.* Toronto: Ontario Teacher's Association.

Association for Media Literacy. (1990). *AML anthology.* Toronto.

Association des cinémas parallèles du Québec. (1991). *Cinémagie.* Montréal: Association des cinémas parallèles du Québec.

Aufderheide, P. (1992). *Media literacy: A report of the national leadership conference on media literacy.* Queenstown, Maryland: The Aspen Institute.

Bantock, G. H. (1952). *Freedom and authority in education: A criticism of modern cultural and education assumptions.* London: Faber.

Barnes, D. R. (1992). *From communication to curriculum* (2nd ed.). Portsmouth, NH: Boynton/Cook.

Barthes, R. (1957). *Mythologies.* Paris: Edition du Seuil.

Barthes, R. (1967). *Elements of semiology.* London: Cape.

Barthes, R. (1977). *Image, music, text.* New York: Hill and Wang.

Bazalgette, C. (Ed.). (1989). *Primary media education: A curriculum statement.* London: British Film Institute.

Bazalgette, C. (1991). *Media education.* London: Hodder and Stoughton.

Beard, H., & Cerf, C. (1993). *The official politically correct dictionary Handbook.* New York: Villard Books.

Berger, G. (1983). *L'education aux medias: Un example de Suisse.* Perspectives, 13 (2), 245-256.

Bogdan, R., & Biklen, S. K. (1998). *Qualitative research for education: An introduction to theory and methods* (3rd ed.). Boston: Allyn and Bacon.

Borge, J. (1985). *Media teacher's handbook, media workbook.* Floriana, Malta: Secretariat for Social Communications.

Borge, J. (1989). *Media studies.* Blata L Blata, Malta: Secretariat for Social Communications.

Boscombe, E. (1974). *Television studies in schools and colleges.* IBA Report. Screen Education.

Boyd Barrett, O., & Braham, P. (Eds.). (1987). *Media, knowledge and power: A reader.* London: Croom Helm.

Bowker, J. (Ed.). (1991). *Secondary media education: A curriculum statement.* London: British Film Institute.

Brandeis, J. (1993). *Media education: Initiative across Canada.* English Quarterly, 25(2&3), 45-46.

British Film Institute. (1989). *Media education and the national curriculum.* London: BFI Discussion Document.

British Film Institute, Center de liaison de l'enseignement et des moyens d'information, Unesco, Conseil de l'Europe (1990). *Nouvelles orientations dans l'éducation aux médias.* Compte rendu du Colloque tenu à Toulouse du 2 au 6 juillet, Londres: British Film Institute.

Britton, J. N. (1970). *Language and learning.* London: Allan Lane.

Britton, J. N. (1975). *The development of writing abilities* (11-18). London: Macmillian.

Bruffee, K. A. (1986). *Social construction, language and the authority of knowledge: A biographical essay.* College English, 48(8), 773 790.

Bryant, J., & Zillmann, D. (1996). Violence and sex in the media. In M. B. Salwen, & D. W. Stacks (Eds.), *An integrated approach to communication theory and research.* Mahwah, N.J.: Lawrence Erlbaum.

Buckingham, D. (1990). *Watching media learning: Making sense of media education.* London: Falmer Press.

Buckingham, D. (1993a). *Children talking television: The making of television literacy.* London: Falmer Press.

Buckingham, D. (1993b). *English and media studies: Making the difference.* English Quarterly, 25 (2 & 3), 8-13.

Buckingham, D., Fraser, P., & Mayman, N. (1990). Stepping into the void: Beginning classroom research in Media Education. In D. Buckingham (Ed.), *Watching media learning: Making sense of media education.* London: Falmer Press.

Buckingham, D., & Sefton-Green, J. (1994). *Cultural studies goes to school.* London: Taylor and Francis.

Buckingham, D., & Sefton Green, J. (1996). *Cultural studies meets action research in the media classroom.* Educational Action Research, 4 (2), 223-243.

Burgess, G. R. (Ed.). (1985a). *Field methods in the study of education.* Philadelphia: Falmer Press.

Burgess, R. G. (Ed.). (1985b). *Strategies of educational research: Qualitative methods.* London: Falmer Press.

Canavan, K. B. (1972). *Mass media education curriculum guideline for primary school year 1-6.* Sydney: Catholic Education Office.

Caron-Bouchard, M., Marcotte, D., & Vesin, S. (1986). *Guide d'animation pour une session de travail sur les dramatiques et sur la publicité.* Montréal: Association nationale des téléspectateurs.

Carpenter, E. S. (1968). *Explorations in communication.* Boston: Beacon Press.

Carpenter, D., Smart, W., & Worsnop, C. (1988). *Media: Images and issues*. Toronto: Addison-Wesley.

Carr, W., & Kemmis, S. (1986). *Becoming critical: Education, knowledge, and action research*. London: Falmer Press.

Center St-Pierre. (1993). *Resources en communication*. Montréal: Author.

Chandler, D. (1998). *The Media and Communication Studies Site: Active Interpretation*. http//www.aber.ac.uk/~dgc/mcs.html.

Cochran Smith, M., & Lytle, S. L. (1993). *Inside/outside: Teacher research and knowledge*. New York: Teachers College Press.

Condie, Richard. (1991) *The Apprentice*. National Film Board of Canada

Considine, D. M., & Haley, G. E. (1992). *Visual messages: Integrating imagery into instruction*. Englewood, Colorado: Teacher Ideas Press.

Corder-Bolz, C. R. (1979). *Elementary school student's critical television viewing skills project*. Austin: Southwest Educational Development Laboratory.

Courts, Patrick, L. (1992). *Literacy and empowerment*. Toronto: OISE Press.

Cowles, K., & Dick, E. (1984). *Teaching media studies: An introduction to methods and resources*. Glasgow: The Scottish Film Council.

Crowther Report. (1959). Vol. 1. London: HMSO

Department of Education and Science. (1975). *A language for life: Report of the committee of inquiry appointed by the Secretary of State for Education and Science under the chairmanship of Sir Alan Bullock F. B. A*. London: Her Majesty's Stationery Office.

Department of Education and Science. (1983). *Popular television and schoolchildren: The report of a group of teachers.* London: Author.

Dewey, J. (1929). *The quest for certainty.* New York: Minton, Balch.

Dewey, J. (1934). *Art as experience.* New York: Minton, Balch.

Dewey, J. (1938). *Experience and education.* New York: Macmillian.

Dias, P. X. (1992). Literary reading and classroom constraints: Aligning practice with theory. In J. Langer (Ed.), *Literature instruction: A focus on student response.* Urbana. Ill.: NCTE.

Dick, E. (1990, May). *A conceptual framework for media education.* Paper presented to the first AML International Conference on Media Education. University of Guelph, Ontario.

Dick, E. (1992). Developing broad strategies and interventions in media education. In M. Alvarado & O. Boyd Barrett (Eds.), *Media education: An introduction* (pp. 408 413), London: British Film Institute in partnership with the Open University.

Dixon, J. (1969). *Growth through English.* Reading, England: Oxford Press.

Doelker, C. (1992). Bildpädagogik - das chronishe Defizit der Medienerziehung. In Bertelsmann Stiftung (Ed.), *Medienkompetenz als Herausforderung an Shule und Bildung: Ein deutsch-amerikanisher Dialog, Kompendium zu einer Konferenz der Bertelsmann Stiftung* (pp. 208-217). Gütersloh: Verlag Bertelsmann Stiftung.

Dominquez, J. (1990). *Activos y creativos con los medios de communicacion social.* Bogata: Ediciones Paulinas.

Donohue. T. (1978). *Television's impact on emotionally disturbed children's value system.* Child Study Journal, 8 (3), 187-345.

Doughty, P. S., Pearce, J., & Thornton, G. (1976). *Language in use* (2nd edition). London: E. Arnold.

Duncan, B. (1988). Mass media and popular culture. Toronto: Harcourt Brace Jovanovich.

Duncan, B. (1993). *Surviving education's desert storms: Adventures in media literacy.* English Quarterly, 25(2 3).

Ellis, M. (1993). *Theory and practical work in Media Education.* English Quarterly, 25(2-3), 28-34.

Emery, W. (1993). *The role of media literacy in teacher training and school curricula: To integrate across the curriculum or create a new discipline?* A Paper Presented at Dawson College, Montreal, Canada.

Emery, W., Anderson, A., Rother, I., Tiseo, F., Mitchell, Luchs, M., C., & Brandeis, J. (1995). *Media Files – Introduction.* Gouvernement du Quebec, Ministere de l'Education.

Ennis, R. (1962). *A concept of critical thinking.* Harvard Educational Review, 32 (1), 81-111.

Far West Laboratory Office of Educational Project. (1980). *Inside television: A guide to critical viewing (teacher's guide, student handbook, worksheet).* Palo Alto: Science & Behavior Books.

Faurie Roudier, A., & Vallet, A. (1983). *Le Langage total: experiences internationales d'education a la communication et aux medias.* Collection, Communication et Siciete, No. 9, Paris: UNESCO.

Ferguson, B. (1981). *Practical work and pedagogy.* Screen Education, 38, 42-55.

Finn, J. D. (1972). *Extending Education Through Technology. Washington: Association for Educational Technology.*

Fiske, J. (1982). *Introduction to communication*. London: Methuen.

Fiske, J. (1989). *Reading the popular*. Boston: Unwin Hyman.

Fiske, J., & Hartley, J. (1978). *Reading television*. London: Methuen.

Freire, P. (1970). *Cultural action for freedom*. Cambridge: Harvard Review.

Freire, P. (1973). *Education for critical consciousness*. New York: Seabury Press.

Freire, P. (1990). *The pedagogy of the oppressed*. New York: Continuum.

Gee, J. P. (1996). *Social linguistics and literacies: Ideology in discourses* (2nd ed.). London: Taylor & Francis.

Gere, A. R. (1992). *Language and reflection: An integrated approach to teaching English*. New York: Macmillian.

Gere, A. R., & Smith, E. (1979). *Attitudes, language, and change*. Urbana, Ill: National Council of Teachers of English.

Gibson, R. (1984). *Structuralism and education*. London: Hodder and Stroughton.

Giroux, H. A. (1983). *Theory and resistance in education: A pedagogy for the opposition*. New York: Bergin and Garvey.

Giroux, H. A., & McLaren, P. (Eds.) (1989). *Critical pedagogy, the state, and cultural struggle*. New York: State University of New York Press.

Glaser, B. G., & Strauss, A. L. (1967). *The discovery of grounded theory: Strategies for qualitative research*. Chicago: Adeline.

Golay, J. P. (1988). *Education aux medias. Actes du Symposium: Educations aux medias.*

Goodson, I. (1987). *School subjects, curriculum and change.* London: Falmer Press.

Grahame, J. (1990). Playtime: Learning about media institutions through practical work. In D. Buckingham (Ed.), *Watching media learning: Making sense of media education* (pp. 101-123). London: Falmer Press.

Gratton, P., & Joncas, L. (1988). *La culture en question: Intervention pédagogique sur la désexisation des apprentissages.* Montréal: Centrale d'enseignement du Québec.

Graves, D. (1983). *Writing: Teachers and children at work.* Exeter, N.H.: Heinemann.

Greene, M. (1988). *Research currents: What are the language arts for?* Language Arts, 65(5), 474 481.

Guba, E., & Lincoln, Y. (1981). *Effective evaluation: Improving the usefulness of evaluation results through responsive and naturalistic approaches.* San Francisco: Jossey Bass.

Half our future (Newsom Report). (1963). Central Advisory Council for Education. London: HMSO.

Hall, S. (1996). Signification, representation, ideology: Althusser and the post structuralist debates. In J. Curran, D. Morley, & V. Walkerdine. *Cultural studies and communications.* London: E. Arnold.

Hall, G. S., & Mansfield, J. M. (1886). *Hints toward a select and descriptive bibliography of education.* Detroit: Gale Research.

Hall, S., & Whannel, P. (1964). *The popular arts*. London: Hutchinson.

Halliday, M. A. (1974). *Language and social man*. London: Longman for the Schools Council.

Halloran, J. D., & Jones, M. (1992). The innoculation approach. In M. Alvarado, & O. Boyd Barrett (Eds.), *Media education: An introduction*. London: BFI Publishing.

Hammersley, M., & Atkinson, P. (1983). *Ethnography, principles in practice*. London: Routledge and Kegan Paul.

Hart, A., & Benson, A. (1994, July). *Researching media education in English classrooms in the U.K.* Paper presented at the First World Meeting on Media Education, La Coruna, Spain.

Heath, S. B. (1983). *Ways with words: Language, life and work in communities and classrooms*. Cambridge: Cambridge University Press.

Heinich, R. (1989). *Instructional media and the new technologies of instruction*. New York: MacMillan.

Hodge, R., & Tripp, D. (1986). *Children and television: A semiotic approach*. Stanford: Stanford University Press.

Hoggart, R. (1959). *The uses of literacy*. London: Chatto and Windus.

Holdaway, D. (1979). *The foundations of literacy*. Sydney: Ashton Scholastic.

Institut Canadien d'Éducation aux Adultes (ICEA) et Centrale d'Enseignement du Québec (CEQ). *Une bonne histoire: Guide d'animation et vidéo d'accompagnement,* Montréal: CEQ.

Institut québécois du cinéma. (1992). *L'éducation cinématographique au Québec: préparer les auditoires de demain,* Montréal: Institut québécois du cinéma.

Jacquinot, G. (1985). *L'ecole devant les ecrans.* Paris: Les editions EDSF.

JES-COM-Philippine, People in Communication (PIC). (1989). *Media kit.* Loyola Heights: Ateneo de Manila University.

Kasai, Yoshikasu. (1987) *Teenage Mutant Ninja Turtles: The Epic Begins.* Murakami-Wolf-Swenson Film Productions.

Kemmis, S. (1988). *Evaluating curriculum.* Geelong, Vic.: Deakin University.

Kemmis, S., & McTaggart, R. (Eds.). (1988). *The action research planner* (3rd ed.). Victoria: Deakin University.

Labarre, L. (1988). *L'éducation aux médias: Une expérience originale en milieu communautaire.* Élan formateur, 1 (3), 5-7.

Lauzon, R. (1985). *Au-delà de l'image.* Montréal: Association nationale des téléspectateurs.

Leavis, F. R., & Thompson, D. (1933). *Culture and environment: The training of critical awareness.* London: Chatto & Windus.

LeCompte. M., Preissle, J., & Tesch, R. (1993). *Ethnography and qualitative design in educational research* (2nd ed). San Diego: Academic Press.

Lehman, R. (1980). *Centering television in the classroom.* Monona: Television Learning.

Leveranz, D., & Tyner, K. (1993). *Inquiring minds want to know: What is media literacy?* The Independent (August/September) (cited at (http//laplaza.org/~cmhshomeHimes3.html).

Lévi-Strauss, C. (1976). *Structural anthropology*. New York: Basic Books.

Livesley, J. (1987). *Media scenes and class acts*. Markham: Pembrooke.

Livesley, J., McMahon, B., Pungente, S. J., & Quin, R. (1990). *Meet the media*. Toronto: Globe-Modern Curriculum.

Lloyd-Kolkin, D., & Tyner, K. (1991). *Media and you: An elementary media literacy curriculum*. Englewood Cliffs, NJ: Educational Technology.

Lusted, D. (Ed.). (1991). *The media studies book: A guide for teachers*. London: Routledge.

Masterman, L. (1980). *Teaching about television*. London: Macmillan.

Masterman, L. (1983a). *Mass media education: Theoretical issues and practical possibilities*. Prospects, 13(2), 183 191.

Masterman, L. (1983b). Media education in the 1980's. *Journal of Educational Television*, 9 (1), 7 12.

Masterman, L. (1985). *Teaching the media*. London: Comedia/MK Press.

Masterman, L. (1990, May). *Key concepts of media education*. Paper presented to the first AML International Conference on Media Education. University of Guelph, Ontario.

Masterman, L. (1991). *An overview of media education in Europe*. Media Development, 1, 3 9.

Masterman, L. (Ed.). (1994). *En Reflechissant sur l'education aux medias. in Le Conseil de L'Europe: L'education aux medias dans L'Europe des annees 90*. Collection Education, Strasbourg: Les editions du Conseil de L'Europe.

Mayher, J. S. (1990). *Uncommon sense: Theoretical practice in language education.* Portsmouth, NH: Boynton/Cook Publishers.

Mayher, J. S. (1991). *Search and re-search: What the inquiring teacher needs to know.* New York: Falmer Press.

McCormick, K., Waller, G., & Flower, L. (1992). *Reading texts: Reading, responding, writing.* Toronto: D.C. Heath and Company.

McKee, R. (1997). *Story.* New York: Regan Books.

McMahon, B., & Quin, R. (1984). *Exploring images.* Melbourne: Bookland.

McMahon, B., & Quin, R. (1985). *Real images: Film and television.* Melbourne: Macmillan.

McMahon, B., & Quin, R. (1987). *Stories and stereotypes.* Melbourne: Longman Cheschire.

McMahon, B., & Quin, R. (1988). *Meet the media.* Melbourne: Macmillan.

McMahon, B., & Quin, R. (1990). *Australian images.* Sydney, Australia: Science Press.

McMahon, B., & Quin, R. (1992). *Monitoring standards in education: Media analysis.* A report prepared for the Ministry of Education, Western Australia.

McNiff, J. (1993). *Teaching as learning: An action research approach.* New York: Routledge.

McTaggart, R. (1997). *Particpatory action research: International contexts and consequences.* Albany: State University of New York Press.

McTaggart, R., & Garbutcheon Singh, M. (1986). *New directions in action research.* Curriculum Perspectives, 6(2), 42 46.

Means, B., Chelemer C., & Knapp, M. S. (1991). Introduction: Rethinking teaching for at-risk students. In B. Means, C. Chelemer, & M. S. Knapp (Eds.), *Teaching advanced skills to at-risk students: Views from research and practice*. San Francisco: Jossey Bass.

Medway, P. (1980). *Finding a language: Autonomy and learning in school*. Readers in Association with Chameleon.

Merriam, S. B. (1988). *Case study research in education: A qualitative approach*. San Francisco: Jossey Bass.

Metz, C. (1977). Images et pédagogie. In C. Metz (Ed.), *Essai sur la signification du cinéma*, Tome II (pp. 141-149). Paris: Klinsiek.

Miles, M. B., & Huberman, A. M. (1984). *Qualitative data analysis: A sourcebook of new methods*. Beverley Hills, CA: Sage.

Ministere de l'Education. (1985). English language arts: *Talking means . . . cycle one and two*. Gouvernment de Quebec. Ministere de l'Education.

Ministere de l'Education. *Direction des edudes economique at demographiques* (1993). Education Indicators for the Elementary and Secondary Levels.

Ministry of Education of Ontario. (1989). *Media literacy, intermediate and senior divisions: resource guide*. Toronto: Queen's Printer for Ontario.

Minkkinen, S. (1978). *A general curricular model for mass media education*. Paris: UNESCO.

Minkkinen, S., & Nodenstreng, K. (1983). *Finlande: plans courageux et serieux problemes*. Perspectives, 13 (2), 237-347.

Moffett, J. (1968). *Teaching the universe of discourse*. Boston: Houghton Mifflin.

Moffett, J., & Wagner, B. J. (1976). *Student-centered language arts and reading, K-13*: A handbook for teachers (2nd ed.). Boston: Houghton Mifflin.

Moore, B. (1991). Media education. In D. Lusted (Eds.), *The media studies book*. London: Routledge.

Muller, H. J. (1967). *The uses of English: Guidelines for the teaching of English*. New York: Holt, Rinehart and Winston.

Murdock, G., & Phelps, G. (1973). *Mass media and the secondary school*. London: MacMillan.

National Film Board of Canada. (1989). *Media and society*. Films recorded into three videotapes. Teacher's guide.

National Film Board of Canada. (1993). *Constructing reality*. Films recorded into three videotapes. Teacher's guide.

New South Wales Department of Education. (1984). *Mass Media Education K-12*. Sydney, Australia: NSW Department of Education.

Nostbakken, D., & Nostbakken, J. (1982). *Guidelines for the power of television workshop project*. Toronto: Children's Broadcast Institute.

Nye, R. B. (1978). Notes on a rationale for popular culture. In J. Nachbar, D. Weiser, & J. L. Wright (Eds.), *A popular culture reader*. Bowling Green: Bowling Green University Popular Press.

Patton, M. Q. (1990). *Qualitative evaluation and research methods* (2nd ed.). Newbury Park, CA: Sage.

Penfield, J. (1987). *The media: Catalysts for communicative language learning*. Reading Mass.: Addison Wesley.

Pierre, E. (1983). *Une experience francaise de formation du jeune telespectateur*. Perspectives, Paris: UNESCO 13 (2), 257-264.

Piette, J. (1992). Teaching television critical viewing skills: From theory to practice to theory. In Bertelsmann Stiftung (Ed.), *Medienkompetenz als Herausforderrung an Shule und Bildung: Ein deutsch americanisher Dialog. Kompenduim zu einer Konferenz der Bertelsmann Stiftung.* Bertelsmann Stiftung.

Piette, J. (1995). *L'operation du concept d'esprit critique dans les programmes d'education aux medias.* Unpublished doctoral dissertation, Department de la communication, Universite de Montreal, Montreal.

Piette, J., Giroux, L., & Caron, A. H. (1986). *Un programme d'éducation critique à la télévision pour les jeunes en milieu de loisir.* Montréal: Université de Montréal, Département de Communication / Association nationale des téléspectateurs.

Ploghoft, M. E., & Anderson, J. A. (1982). *Teaching critical television viewing skills: An integrated approach.* Springfield, Illinois: Charles C. Thomas.

Postman, N. (1971). *The soft revolution: A student handbook for turning schools around.* New York: Delacorte Press.

Postman, N. (1982). *The disappearance of childhood.* New York: Delacorte Press.

Postman, N. (1995). *The end of education.* New York: Vintage Books.

Potter, R. L., Faith, C., Ganek, L. B. (1979). *Channel: Critical reading/TV viewing skills.* Freeport, New York: Educational activities.

Potter, R. L., Hanneman, C. E., & Faith, C. (Eds). (1980). *TV readers skills kit.* Freeport, New York: Educational activities.

Potter, R. L., Hanneman, C. E., & Faith, C. (1981). Television behind the scene: Teachers guide. In R. L. Potter, C. E. Hanneman, & C. Faith (Eds.), *TV readers skills kit.* New York: Educational activities.

Propp, V. (1968). *Morphology of the folktale* (2nd ed). Austin: University of Texas Press.

Purves, A. C., Rogers, T., & Sotler, A. C. (1990). *How porcupines make love II: Teaching a response-centered literature curriculum.* New York: Longman.

Quebec Service Generale des Communications du Ministere de L'Education. (1979). *The schools of Quebec: Policy statement and plan of action: Children with learning difficulties and adaptation.* Author.

Quin, R. (1993). *Teaching media: Paradigms for future instruction.* Paper presented at Madison National English Teachers Association.

Quin, R., & McMahon, B. (1993). *Teaching the context: Another dimension to media education.* Paper presented at Seattle Media Arts Conference.

Rosenblatt, L. (1968). *Literature as exploration.* New York: Modern Language Association of America.

Rosenblatt, L. (1978). *The reader, the text and the poem.* Carbondale: University Press.

Rother, I. L. (1986). *Using video as a process tool with learning disabled and emotionally disturbed adolescents.* Unpublished master's thesis, Concordia University, Montreal.

Rother, I. L. (1992). The apprentice. *Animando to Zea,* 6 (2), 6-7.

Saettler, L. P. (1990). *The evolution of American educational technology.* Englewood: Libraries Unlimited.

Sanjek, R. (1990). *Fieldnotes: The making of anthropology.* Ithaca: Cornell University Press.

Schon, D. (1983). *The reflective practitioner: How professionals think in action.* New York: Basic Books.

Schon, D. (1987). *Educating the reflective practitioner: Toward a new design for teaching and learning in the professions.* San Francisco: Jossey Bass.

Scottish Film Council. (1990a). *Local heroes - resource pack.* Glasgow: Author.

Scottish Film Council. (1990b). *Picturing women - resource pack.* Glasgow: Author.

Scrimshaw, P. (1992). Evaluating media education through action research. In M. Alvarado, & O. Boyd Barrett (Eds.), *Media Education.* London: British Film Institute.

Secondary School Curriculum: English Language Arts I-V. (1982). Gouvernement du Quebec, Ministere de L'Éducation. Direction generale du développement pédagogie. Document no. 16 - 3236.

Shayer, D. (1972). *The teaching of English in schools 1900-1970.* London: Boston Routledge & Kegan Paul.

Shepherd, R. (1993). *Elementary media education: The perfect curriculum.* English Quarterly, 25 (2-3), 35-38.

Shor, I., & Freire, P. (1987). *A pedagogy for liberation: Dialogs on transforming education.* South Hadley, Mass: Bergin & Garvey.

Silverblatt, A. (1995). *Media literacy: Keys to interpreting media messages.* London: Praeger.

Singer, D. G., Singer, J. L., & Zuckerman, D. M. (1981a). *Getting the most Out of TV.* Santa Monica: Goodyear Publishing Book.
Singer, D. G., Singer, J. L., & Zuckerman, D. M. (1981b). *Teaching television: How to use TV to your child's advantage.* New York: The Dial Press.

Smart, W. (Ed.). (1992). *The AML anthology/supplement.* Toronto: Association for Media Literacy.

Smith, F. (1988). *Joining the literacy club: Further essays into education.* Portsmouth, N.H: Heinemann.

Solsken, J. W. (1993). *Literacy, gender and work.* New Jersey: Albex.

South Australia Education Department. (1983a). *R-12 media lab.* Adelaide: Government Printer, South Australia.

South Australia Education Department. (1983b). *R-12 media studies.* Adelaide: Government Printer, South Australia.

South Australia Education Department. (1984a). *R-7 media lab.* Adelaide: Government Printer, South Australia.

South Australia Education Department. (1984b). *8-12 media lab.* Adelaide: Government Printer, South Australia.

Stafford, R. (1990). Redefining creativity: Extended project work in GCSE media studies. In D. Buckingham (Ed.), *Watching media learning: Making sense of media education* (pp. 81-100). London: Falmer Press.

Stainback, S., Stainback, W., & Forest, M. (Eds.). (1989). *Educating all students in the mainstream of regular education.* Baltimore: P.H. Brookes.

Strauss, A., & Corbin, J. (1990). *Basics of qualitative research: Grounded theory procedures and techniques.* London: Sage.

Street, B. V. (1984). *Literacy in theory and practice.* New York: Syndicate of the University of Cambridge.

Thoman, E. (1990). *Connect: Quarterly Magazine Newsletter for members of the Center for Media and Values.*

Thomas, J. (1993). *Doing critical ethnography.* Newbury Park, Calif: Sage.

Trudel, L. (1992). *La population face aux médias*. Montréal: VLB éditeur.

Tulodziecki, G. (1992). Medienerziehung las facherubergreifende und integrative Auf gabe. In B. Stiftung (Ed.), *Medienkompetenz als Herausforderung an Shule und Bildung: Ein deutsch amerikanisher Dialog, Kompendium zu einer Konferenz der Bertelsmann Stiftung* (pp. 311-322). Gutersloh: Verlaf Bertelsmann Stiftung.

UNESCO. (1972). *International meeting of media teachers*. Mannheim.

UNESCO. (Ed.). (1977). *L'étude des médias dans l'enseignement*. Paris: UNESCO.

UNESCO. (Ed.). (1982). *Education and the media: Trends, issues, prospects: An international symposium on educating users of mass media*. German Commission for UNESCO, Munich: Institut für Film und Bild in Wissenschaft und Unterict, 18-22.

UNESCO. (Ed.). (1983). *Numéro spécial "L'éducation aux médias"*. Perspectives, 13 (2).

UNESCO. (Ed.). (1984). *L'éducation aux médias*. Paris: UNESCO.

UNESCO. (1989). *The plan of action to eradicate illiteracy by the year 2000*. General Conference, Twenty-fifth session, Paris. (Document 25c/71).

Urgerleider, C., & Jacques, R. D. (1980). *Media education workshop: Happy days*, Victoria.

Vanderstichelen, F., & Guyot, J. C. (Eds.). (1989). *Tout savoir sur la Télé*. Bruxelles: Media Animation-Médialogue.

Vygotsky, L. S. (1978). *Mind in society: The development of higher psychological processes*. Cambridge: Harvard University Press.

Williamson, J. (1981). *How does girl number 20 understand ideology?* Screen Education, 40, 80-87.

Willinsky, J. (1991). *Postmodern literacy: A primer.* Interchange, 22(4), 56-76.

Winn, M. (1985). *The plug-in drug* (rev. ed.). New York, N.Y: Penguin.

Worsnop, C. M. (1994). *Screening images.* Mississauga: Wright Communications.

Wright, J. C., Watkins, B. A., & Huston Stein, A. (1978). *Active versus passive television viewing: A model of the development of television information processing by children.* Center for Research on the Influence of Children (CRITC), First annual Report to the Spenser Foundation. Research Report No. 10.

Yin, R. K. (1994). *Case study research: Design and methods.* Thousand Oaks, CA: Sage.

IRVING LEE ROTHER, PH.D

Dr. Rother is a multi-award winning English Language Arts Media Education educator with thirty-one years of experience teaching, consulting, and designing curriculum at the school, university, and provincial levels. He was a member of a provincial commission on transforming classroom culture through integrating English Language Arts, literacy, and ICT into curriculum, as well as using multi-media technologies to enhance teaching and learning, with an emphasis on at-risk high school students. He has participated in a wide range of curriculum review and development initiatives at primary, secondary, and teacher education levels. In 1990, Dr. Rother co-founded and was co-president of the Association for Media Education in Quebec. He was also a founding member of the Canadian Association for Media Education Organizations. Dr. Rother has been a lecturer at McGill University, Bishop's University, and the University of Hong Kong; he is often asked to speak about his work at various conferences across Canada and abroad. In recent years he was one of six Media Educators from the West to participate in the First International Media Education Conference in

Beijing, China. Dr. Rother has also volunteered his expertise in the West Bank, Nigeria, and South Africa. Currently, Dr. Rother is program developer, head teacher of the Alternative Career Education Program in Lake of Two Mountains High School in Deux Montagnes, Quebec, one of many schools in the Sir Wilfrid Laurier School Board, where his mandate includes use of ICT, literacy, English Language Arts, and Media Education in alternative education programs.

COLOPHON

As there is a stunning array of ways to create meaning – which this book's exploration of media makes clear – so there is a stunning variety of letterforms used to convey meaning in a print text such as this one. The typefaces used to communicate *The Struggle for Literacy*'s meaning to you, the reader, have been carefully chosen.

The majority of the typefaces used in this book are contemporary in design, to reflect the modern approach to literacy described in the book. These contemporary typefaces were all designed by Jos Buivenga of Arnhem, the Netherlands. They are: *Anivers* (2008), used for the title page and for decorative elements, such as the asterisk; *Delicious* (1994-1996), used in its various forms for the tables; *Fontin* (2004) appears in the sub-headings; *Fontin Sans* (2007) was used to set the captions; *Museo* (2008) appears in the chapter titles; and the body of the text is set in *Tallys* (2006). All these fonts and more can be found at the *ExlJbris* type foundry: *www.josbuivenga.demon.nl*

The caption on page twenty-seven is set in *IM Fell de Walpergen Pica Pro*. This typeface was cut by Peter de Walpergen and acquired by John Fell in 1692. The Fell Types were digitally reproduced by Igino Marini. *www.iginomarini.com*